for Katie

We are together
in spirit +
with love and
blessings D.

Kindling Spirit

HEALING FROM WITHIN

CARL HAMMERSCHLAG, M.D.

Kindling Spirit. © 2011, Carl Hammerschlag, M.D.

Digitally Published by Turtle Island Press, Phoenix, AZ

Library of Congress Cataloging-in-Publication Data
Hammerschlag MD CPAE, Carl.
        Kindling Spirit
Inspiration, health, wellness, thought
I. Hammerschlag Carl II.   III. Title

Table of Contents

Dedication

For Elaine, my beloved wife of 50
never-boring years. Here's looking at
you, Sweetheart, and still seeing you
for the first time.

Foreword

I am a physician; my specialty is psychiatry. I have spent my whole life trying to figure out what's reality, how to separate science from superstition, and how to understand the healing mystery. My practice has been a departure from conventional medicine. I spent the first 20 years working exclusively with Native Americas, first as a general practitioner and later as Chief of Psychiatry at the Phoenix Indian Medical Center.

I've written about that transformational journey from medical doctor to healer in my earlier books. That journey began as the first-born son of Holocaust survivors, raised in a traditional Jewish home in the Washington Heights section of Manhattan during World War II. The history of my ancestors has been a seminal influence in my life and accounts for my identification with the downtrodden and my abiding mistrust of people and institutions in entrenched positions of power.

DR. H AND HIS MOTHER

I was a child of the '60s, involved in civil rights demonstrations and protestations against the war. When I graduated from medical school, I joined the Indian Health Service as my alternative to going to Vietnam. I thought I'd go for a couple of years, serve my obligatory time, and then move on with the rest of my life. But that experience turned out to be the rest of my life. Working with American Indians changed my life. They challenged my medical school assumptions about how people got sick and how they got well.

As a Western-trained scientist, I believed everything could be explained. Even if we didn't know the answers now, sooner or later we'd discover them. I believed there was a logical, direct, and causal relationship that explained all natural phenomena.

As a physician, I believed in evidence-based medicine. Basically, show me the reproducible facts and that will determine my practice. In Indian Country, I got to meet a few traditional healers, a term I use interchangeably with "medicine men" or "shamans." They looked at my medical genius, the diagnostic machines, and sophisticated surgery, in awesome disbelief because what I saw as scientific, they saw as magic. When I saw what the medicine men did, I thought that was magical, but they saw their practice as perfectly

1

logical and explainable. They watched animals heal their bloody and infected wounds by rubbing against certain trees and bushes that healed them. The traditional healers used those same plants when they were wounded. Of course, they spent a lot of time studying those animals and plants. Interestingly, all modern pharmaceuticals are rooted in plants that shamans have known about for centuries.

I studied psychiatry at Yale, but I learned a whole new way of seeing into a patient's mind when I returned to Indian Country. I learned ways other than empathic listening to open a patient's mind. In addition, I learned how to induce trance states by dancing, drumming, and chanting and about the use of psychodynamically-powerful drugs to open channels of the unconscious mind. I was interested in working with traditional healers to help provide me with some framework to understand the cultural myths and stories that my patients believed could make them sick.

"I learned ways other than empathic listening to open a patient's mind."

My credibility with traditional healers had nothing to do with my degrees and credentials. Instead, they wanted to know things about my relationship with my father, if could I dance, and if I could sing in my own tribal language. The most important consideration in their helping me to learn was that they did not hold my degrees against me. I had diplomas hanging on my walls, but that didn't mean I knew anything about healing. There were no degrees dangling from my ceiling or embedded in the floor, but that didn't mean there was nothing to be learned by looking up or looking down.

I watched shamans remove blood clots from bellybuttons, elk teeth from armpits, as well as place hot coals in their mouths and blow the sparks onto a patient's sick body. If a psychotic patient did not respond to my words and drugs, I referred them to a medicine man. For example, I once saw a young pregnant woman with a fixed delusional system. She believed her unborn child had died in her womb, and even though she could hear its heart beating, she believed it was now turning into tar, small pieces of which were clogging her blood vessels. In this psychotic state, she tried to get her dead baby out by sticking cigarettes into her bellybutton. Her symptoms began shortly after she saw a hummingbird fly into her bedroom, and in its frantic attempt to escape, break its neck behind a mirror. I gave her drugs, which sedated her into complete isolation but didn't stop her delusions.

I asked a medicine man what this could be about, and he explained that the dead bird was her clan totem and its death a message that some disaster would befall her. I asked him what he would do to treat her condition, and he said he would perform a ceremony in which he would be able to see inside her and get the dead bird out. The Indian Health Service paid a consulting fee to support this all-night ceremony, during which the healer showed her the feathers he had extricated from her belly. Afterward, she got better and I was awed.

Slowly, I came to understand the similarity between my psychiatric language —symptomatic behaviors caused by trauma to the psyche and the incorporation of negative introjects — and the unconscious forces that get inside and take us over. They are all another name for evil spirits, demons, and witchcraft.

Memories and traumatic events can get inside of us and eat us apart. Those that get inside early in our lives are harder to get out later on. As Plato once instructed, the more ways you can find to help people get rid of what's killing them from within, the better you can heal them. However, it was only when I studied with Milton Erickson, a genius psychiatrist whom I never learned of in my psychiatric training, that I understood how many ways there are to open channels into the unconscious mind.

> "There is a difference between healing and curing."

Having discovered that healing is essentially a spiritual expedition, not a physical one, I now incorporate traditional healing methods in my clinical practice. There is a difference between healing and curing. Healing takes place at the soul level, and the process has less to do with getting better than it does with getting real. Healing is about learning to play the hand you've been dealt rather than asking for a new deal.

It's been more than 10 years since my last book. I'd thought I'd said everything that I had to say and that saying anymore would be redundant. But I'm aging, and the person I spent so much time developing is not the man I am now. No matter how much time I spend trying to keep doing what I always have been, something reminds me that I can't; my bladder pleads at night, my bones click, and I forget why I came into the kitchen. I preach about staying open and that change is good, but sometimes it's hard for me to keep an open mind. Sometimes it's hard to see what was once familiar in a new way.

I'm going to tell you some stories about my own healing journey, about the struggles, the triumphs, and even the occasional enlightenments. Even though I may have nothing new to say, the old material still needs to get reworked because there are always new endings to the old stories.

All insight is a matter of perspective, a willingness to look at the familiar in a new way. I've learned that there is a spiritual aspect to healing. Spiritual, mind you, not religious. Religions are bridges to the spirit, and there are many bridges all leading to the same destination.

This is my story. I'm hoping you might see pieces of your own and be encouraged to embark on your journey of discovery. Kindling the spirit, that ineffable quality to move beyond what we once thought were limitations, is what will allow us to undertake that journey, see the familiar in a new way, and write new chapters to our lives.

Chapter 1

Looking Again At What You Know

didn't learn about health in medical school.

I learned a lot about disease and how to diagnose and treat it. When I finished my training, I couldn't wait to apply my newly developed skills on adoring patients. I wanted them to trust in me and believe that I had their best interests at heart. I was familiar with the most current diagnostic tools and treatment options, and all they had to do was to place themselves in my hands and let me do it to them.

In my first book, The Dancing Healers, I told the story about an old Pueblo Indian man, Santiago, who taught me how to dance. I met Santiago during morning rounds when he was a patient at the Santa Fe Indian Hospital. Santiago had been admitted through the emergency room the night before, and when I was introduced as his doctor, he looked me up and down and asked where I learned how to heal. I thought he meant where I'd gone to medical school and received my training, so I recited my litany of academic achievement. When I finished, he asked if I knew how to dance. I looked at him, wide-eyed, and asked incredulously, "Do I know how to dance?" He nodded and said, "If you can't dance, you can't heal." Humoring him, I did a little hip-hop at the bedside, which he found amusing. Then I asked him if he knew how to dance. At that time, I did not know he was a traditional medicine man. He said he did, and with the oxygen tube in his nostrils and an IV in his arm, he got up and proceeded to do a Corn Dance with vocals at the bedside.

> "If you can't dance, you can't heal."
>
> - Santiago

When he got back into bed, I asked him if he would teach me to dance that way. He looked at me and said, "I can teach you my steps, but you have to be able to hear your own music." I realized that the ways in which I understood or treated the sick may not be the only or most effective ways. In Indian Country, I learned to listen and look again at the many ways to heal.

I worked exclusively with Native Americans for 20 years because I kept seeing more ways to do the healing dance. Every time I thought, "Now I've got it," something would happen to make me step back and see the familiar in a new way. Nobody gets it; we're always getting it again and again. The key to all growth is to be willing to look at what you thought you knew from another perspective. Certainty is a tribute to arrogance and fear, but it's so much easier to hang on to your preconceptions than making the necessary changes. I had to break my back with multiple surgeries before I gave up competitive athletics. I require repetitive bludgeoning and more suffering and pain before I move beyond my old certainties.

The most difficult preconception for me to give up has been my feelings about Germans. I am the first-born son of Holocaust survivors, and that history has been a constant influence throughout my life. My parents escaped from Germany in 1936 and settled in Manhattan along with 100,000 other German-Jewish refugees, including Dr. Henry Kissinger and Dr. Ruth Westheimer. I was born in 1939 and spoke only German until I was 5 years old. I always understood that I was not a German; I was a Jew from Germany and all those people were complicit in the annihilation of my bloodlines.

As soon as my family learned English, we spoke German only among our relatives. As an adolescent, if I heard Germans speaking German in an elevator, I would ride beyond my stop certain that if I waited long enough, I would catch them in some anti-Semitic slur. We bought no German products and would not sit in a German-made car.

> "When you see yourself reflected in some-one else's eyes, you are forced to face the truth of your own judge-mentalism."

When I came to Indian Country, I had a chance to see myself just as I saw Germans. Native people looked at me and saw just another white man. I wasn't the fellow-sufferer and kindred spirit for which I fancied myself. I may have been a good doctor, but I was still a white man. At some deep unconscious level, I too was responsible for the sins and depredations foisted upon them one hundred years ago. When you see yourself reflected in someone else's eyes, you are forced to face the truth of your own judgementalism. That experience began my journey from doctor to healer. I learned that you can't be a healer if you walk around with that much anger. If I were ever to move toward my own healing, I knew I had to go to Germany and face my monsters. I was 40 years old. Carrying the dislike, distrust, and basketfull of resentments for all those years was crushing my spirit. The time had come; it was now or never.

My wife and I took the super-ferry from England to Belgium where we picked up the train. At the border, crisply uniformed Germans replaced the casually dressed Belgian conductors. It didn't take a millisecond before my old mistrust and fear emerged. My vision of Germans as orderly, clean, efficient, racist, and murderous was an unconscious demon that didn't take long to appear.

In my first few days in Germany, I was guarded. I didn't snarl, but I was standoffish. I'd been in the country a week when I heard an anti-Semitic remark. I've told this story in detail in The Theft of the Spirit, about being in a public park where a young juggler/comedian was entertaining a circle of about one hundred people. Riding a unicycle, he juggled everything from fire to fruits, which he also ate, all the while delivering a hilarious comedic rap. He was juggling grapefruits, catching them with his palms facing downward, when he said: "Wenn Juden es so gemacht haette, dann waere die geschichte der welt veraendert." In translation, he said, "If Jews had learned how to juggle this way, the whole history of civilization would be different." The audience laughed, but I didn't. I didn't know what it meant, but I knew it wasn't funny. A lightning bolt of anger shot up my spine.

After he finished, he passed around the hat and said something to encourage contributions. I waited until everyone left and then walked up to him, still feeling the coursing rage. I told him that something he had said upset me greatly. He looked at me quizzically and asked what he'd said. "When you were juggling those grapefruits," I said. "What did I say?" He asked pleadingly.

I told him, and then nodding in recognition he said: "Ich habe nicht Juden gesagt. I didn't say Juden. Ich habe Newton gesagt." I said Newton, Sir Isaac Newton. If Newton had learned how to juggle upside down, he would never have discovered the laws of gravity."

In German, the words sound almost identical. He said "Newton," but I heard "Juden." I heard what I wanted to hear, what I was prepared to hear, so that I could keep seeing and believing what I once thought I knew. In the old days, I would have left right after I'd heard what I perceived to be an anti-Semitic crack. Had I left, I would have taken only my old certainties with me, which had nothing to do with reality. I could have kept seeing and doing the things I had always seen and done.

I hugged him and thanked him for helping me to continue to do my work. At that moment, I didn't feel like a fool for some reason. My mistake seemed to open up a place in my mind that needed illumination. This is how healing happens; you look at something that you thought you knew and then suddenly you see that old certainty from another perspective. All growth is a matter of perspective, looking again at what you thought you knew and seeing it differently.

I needed to look again at my old certainties if I were ever going to come to peace with my unremitting anger and judgment toward Germans. I needed to look at my prejudice toward Germans over and over again. The illumination grows dim from time to time, and we need a rekindling of the healing spirit to continue the healing process. Because of the juggler, I have returned to Germany regularly to teach and to continue to learn how to open up more and keep healing myself. The healing task of our lives is to keep on looking at what's familiar with new eyes.

In 2004, I returned for my yearly visit a week after my mother died. My mother had been in chronic congestive heart failure for years, and with escalating symptoms, her doctor hospitalized her. My wife and I were planning on vacationing in Italy the following week. The new medications failed to improve her, and the day before our anticipated departure, my mother called and said, "I hope you won't be angry with me if I'm not here when you return." I knew my mother pretty well, and this was as close as she could come to asking me not to go. I felt my breath catch in my throat. I believe in inner voices that speak to us, and the one within me knew I couldn't leave her now.

We cancelled our plans and went to see her in a Southern California hospital room. My diminutive 5-foot-2-inch mama seemed even smaller. She was hooked up to IVs and oxygen, and she still labored to breathe. We sat by her bedside as she described her previous night, gasping for breath and hallucinating. She said, "When the only thing I have to look forward to in life is my next breath, then living no longer makes sense. I don't want to live this way. I want to stop these medicines. They're not helping and make me feel worse."

"for the first time since I was child, I did not turn my head away to hide my tears."

She told this to her longtime physician when he came by to make evening rounds. When she finished, Dr. Rudy assured her that she was calling the shots and that he could stop her heart medications and only give her what made feel comfortable. It took a while before the orders were transcribed, and during this time, my mother gave Elaine the last ring from her finger. Running her hand through her hair, she asked how I thought she looked. I told her she looked beautiful, and then she motioned for me to bend down. I am 6 feet 6 inches tall, so I sat down for her to place her hands on my head. She recited the Jewish mother's Sabbath blessing to her son: "May you be like the prophets Ephraim and Manasseh...a source of blessing and pride." By now, she could barely catch her breath after only a couple of words. When she finished, she whispered in my ear, "Will you still call me every Shabbat even when I'm not here?" I promised her that I would, and for the first time since I was child, I did not turn my head away to hide my tears.

They gave her morphine to keep her comfortable, and she nodded off periodically. It was after midnight, and we talked in that special, nothing-left-to-lose intimacy as we were alone. They kept her comfortable, and she rarely aroused herself as her breathing became more irregular. In her sleep, I sang to her a beautiful Hasidic melody she loved, one about crossing a narrow bridge without fear. I sang it over and over and knew she was singing it to me. She died

Looking Again at What You Know

in my hands.

The Hopi Indians believe that one's last breath becomes a cloud, a rain-giving symbol of everlasting life. Every newborn cloud embodies the spirit of your relatives. After they came for her body, I walked out of the hospital into the cool night air and looked up at the night sky to see if she was there.

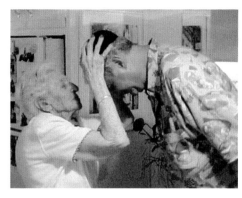

The week after my mother's funeral, I went to Germany to conduct a workshop for mental health professionals, which began on a Friday afternoon. It started with a lecture and moved into an experiential exercise. Participants sat in a traditional Native American talking circle. Everyone would have an opportunity to speak without interruption and spontaneously from the heart without thinking about what they were going to say beforehand.

By the time it came full-circle back to me, it was dark and the Sabbath had arrived. The workshop was being held in a building just across the street from where the town's only synagogue stood until its closure in 1938. I was moved to speak about what it was like to be in Germany at this moment. I told them of my mother's death the week before. I told them she loved the Germany of her childhood and knew the difference between Germans and Nazis long before I had. As I talked about her, I could feel my tears welling up. I stood up saying I wanted to recite Kaddish, the traditional mourner's prayer, for my mother here in her homeland. When I rose to my feet, the whole audience stood with me. The tears, which I have always kept tightly wrapped in public, flowed freely. I promised my mother I would call her on Shabbat, and here I was in Germany, surrounded by Germans who were standing with me.

A couple days later, at the workshop's conclusion, I told the group I felt fortunate to be with them at this special time and asked for their blessing in continuing to do my healing work. I pulled my chair into the middle of the circle and invited anyone who wanted to come forward to place their German hands on my head and give me a blessing.

I sat with my eyes closed, hands opened on my lap, and one by one, dozens came forward to place their hands on me and bless me. Some offered scriptural blessings, others poems, some spoken words, and others songs. When I felt no more hands, I opened my eyes and looked up to find myself surrounded by the group. Fifty people had joined hands in the circle and begun to dance in a circle while singing "Hava Nagila" in Hebrew. I was overwhelmed and could feel the tears flow again. As they danced around me, I stood up and danced in the middle. Slowly the circle spiraled inward until I was hugged in a communal embrace, and then they moved out and danced around me again. In that moment, I swear I saw my mother smile and felt my spirit lift. Love, not time, heals all wounds.

Before I left, Brigitta, a psychologist, came up to me and said, "You know that juggler story you told? I think I know who the juggler is." I told Brigitta that I didn't know his name and couldn't even describe his face anymore, but she said the way I had described him eating apples while juggling on a unicycle was unique, and she actually knew such a guy. She wanted to check it out. I said that'd be great and to let me know what she found. By the time I flew home, it had dropped from my consciousness. Brigitta wrote to me that she'd found one of his old teachers, and when she told him my story, he said that it sounded very much like Holger "Ernst" Riekers. He had dropped out of the university and became a well-known street performer. She said perhaps I would remember his signature closing to every performance. When he would pass the hat around, he would always say, "Don't just throw in coins, because I'm not using the money to make telephone calls. This is how I make a living." When Brigitta wrote this to me, I remembered it immediately and also that I hadn't laughed, because at that point, I had been so angry with him. Ernst was the guy.

"I was a very angry man, with bitterness in my heart, even for your father,"

The teacher said Ernst married, had two children, and then developed stomach cancer and died four years ago at age 41. At the teacher's suggestion, she got in touch with his widow, Anne, and shared the whole story. Anne said it would be nice to have a chance to meet me when I came back to Germany, especially to tell his daughters something about him.

The following year, I met Anne in a café in Muenster. She brought her two young daughters, Amalia and Cecilia, with her on the train from Bremer-haven. My childhood command of the German language was perfect for their age, and I told them their father once saved my life. "I was a very angry man, with bitterness in my heart, even for your father," I told them. I told the whole story about the grapefruits and how he showed me another way of hearing the music. Most importantly, I told them of how it helped to heal me. "Because of your father," I said to them, "I have come back to Germany again and again."

But our stories never end with just our telling of it. The healing journey always continues in ways we may not even realize. I received a letter from Brigitta sharing her side of the story and proving that the story goes on in an endless circle. Here is her side of the story:

When I received the information on your workshop in Rottweil, I was interested since I was looking for input on how to add more soul to my work as a counsellor/therapist. It seemed that someone who had worked with Native Americans might have something interesting to offer. I asked my friend Baer-bel to come along, and we were both quite curious and at the same time a bit sceptical when we took the 10-hour train ride from Oldenburg in northern Germany to Rottweil in southern Germany.

When I heard you present the story about meeting the juggler, I immediately thought of a guy who had attended the same school with me in Bremerhaven. I had very much liked his humor and wit, which were so distinct that I wondered whether he was the same person. But then I had been so absorbed by the un-folding workshop that I put that thought aside for a long time.

About a year later, while attending a conference and visiting my former host family in L.A., the question of the juggler's identity popped up again. I wrote a letter to you letting you know that I had a picture of a juggler that might be the one you had met in Kassel and we arranged to meet. You didn´t recognize him from the photograph which had been about 20 years old, so you asked if I could find out his name and address.

Back in Germany, I wrote a letter to my old school in Bremer-haven hoping there might still be a teacher working there who had known the juggler as a student. And we were lucky! I re-ceived a phone call from Karl-Heinz Ruschke, the juggler´s for-mer teacher and advisor. He told me all he knew about Holger Ernst Riekers, which I passed on to you in my letter. We found out that Ernst had developed stomach cancer and died in 2002 leaving behind his wife and two little daughters.

What really touched me when talking to Karl-Heinz Ruschke was his suggestion that you tell Anne and her children about your encounter with their Ernst, so that the healing circle would be closed; that is something quite unusual for a German teacher to say, and it seemed so wonderfully true. I felt there was an immediate deep understanding between Karl-Heinz Ruschke and myself of the meaning of this story and a recognition of the healing power it inherited. There is this hope to leave something behind that touches the hearts of our children and grandchil-dren in a way that helps them live a good life and gives us some sort of continuity beyond death. In Rottweil, you said, "We will all come and go – what we leave behind is the essence of our soul." In hearing your story, Ernst's children could get a glimpse of the essence of his soul. What an awe-some gift!

As I recognized Ernst by his sense of humor, it turned out you recognized him by his closing line he used when passing around a hat. Thereafter, we were

There is this hope to leave something be-hind that touches the hearts of our children and grandchildren in a way that helps them live a good life and gives us some sort of continuity beyond death.

- Brigitta

sure that Holger Ernst Riekers was the juggler you had seen. You took the relay baton and were enthusiastic about telling the story to Ernst's wife and daughters. We both agreed it would be great to have such a conversation occur face-to-face. And so I contacted Anne to check the possibilities.

It turned out that Anne liked the idea of meeting you very much. She let me know she had experienced a lot of people withdrawing after Ernst's death, perhaps struggling to relate to her and feeling uncomfortable talking about him. For Anne, it felt good to hear someone speaking about Ernst and to talk about him herself. She also considered it very important for her two young daughters to hear stories of their father.

For me, it was amazing and moving to speak with Anne and experience a very intimate connection with someone I didn't even know.

On a hot day in June 2006, we did meet with Anne and her daughters Amalia and Cecilia in Muenster. I felt there was no other alternative than doing my share to complete the healing circle. In some miraculous way, I also felt that I was connected to you, Ernst, and his wife, Anne, and children. My connection made possible the connection between you, Anne, Amalia, and Cecilia. I felt a tremendous joy during those wonderful moments as you, Anne and the children met, and I saw the giving and receiving of love and acceptance. The healing Ernst began in you came full circle as you gave it back to his children.

To me, it seemed as if Amalia and Cecilia soaked in the atmosphere and all that was said. After we had split, Anne and I took the children to a park. At a waterfall, Amalia and Cecilia threw flowers into the water saying, "This flower is for you, Mami, and this one's for you, Papa," thus creating their own ritual of including him. It touched my heart how very present their father's love was for them and how aware they were of the meaning and importance of our meeting. It seemed to have a soothing, comforting effect on them.

More than a year later, when I visited Anne and her daughters, I could see that both Amalia and Cecilia had a vivid memory of you and of our meeting from the previous summer. I was told Amalia liked looking at your website every once in a while and also told other people about you. It seems that hearing you talk about their father has had a lasting impact on them.

This whole experience fills me with awe as I humbly realize there is something greater than ourselves, a power that connects everything in ways we may never completely understand. First, I thought my coming to Rottweil in 2004 was about learning something new and broadening my horizon as a therapist,

> It's been a profound spiritual experience to see the connection in all of us and that of a greater power and the energies that balance to two. Being aware of and a part of that balance has helped me on my own journey of growth and healing.
>
> - Brigitta

Looking Again at What You Know

which it actually did in ways I hadn't imagined. Then it seemed as if I was meant to be there to make this connection possible. Just imagine the likelihood of someone being in your workshop who had gone to the same school as the juggler you had seen 20 years before and then recognizing him through your story.

I liked your poetic remark that, "We are the language of the creative source." For me, this has been an awesome experience of being this language, being written out in the book of life. It's been a profound spiritual experience to see the connection in all of us and that of a greater power and the energies that balance to two. Being aware of and a part of that balance has helped me on my own journey of growth and healing. One can be in a serendipitous moment and have it pass by unnoticed, or one can choose to step out of the familiar, take a risk, and have something new happen where one doesn't know it's outcome. Doing so has given more colour to my life and has made it unfold in ways for which I had long hoped. Since 2004, I've changed my job twice for the better, and I've found my soul mate. I believe the ongoing process of learning that started with your workshop in Rottweil and the experience of finding Ernst, has given me the energy and courage to take all those leaps of faith that have brought me to where I am today.

The evolving story, the opening up my heart and giving without expectations, has returned plenty-fold and has made others open their hearts as well. Now I know that when I make a leap of faith and risk sharing my soul, it's very likely that people will resonate with me and reach out, enhancing my capacity to give and receive love. It has brought me closer to realizing what really counts in life.

This whole experience of finding Ernst has also been about healing through connections. The healing that had begun in the son of Holocaust survivors, through your encounter with the Ernst, was passed on in the resulting connections of you, Anne, and me. I think of my parents, who were born 1925 and 1927, still marked from their traumatic experiences during World War II and their feelings of being misled and taken advantage of in Nazi-Germany. From their point of view, the Nazis misused their enthusiastic idealism as youngsters. The collapse of the Third Reich had left them with huge disappointment, tremendous feelings of shame, and complete bewilderment. They felt betrayed. My mother always told us that if she would have known more, had been more educated, she probably would have realized how the Nazis had manipulated and distorted her thinking. That's why she decided to get as much education and to learn as much as she could after the war was over. She also emphasized learning and developing an independent mind in the upbringing of my three siblings and me. She always encouraged us to look behind ideas and to analyze and question everything. She encouraged us to come to our own conclusions, to not to be lured into something and to be very sceptical toward mass-phenom-

enon. When we challenged her, I remember her quoting Goethe, "die Geister, die ich rief, werd´ ich nicht mehr los." (I can't get rid of the ghosts that call to me.) It must have been exhausting for her, but she smiled as she said it.

To help you find Ernst and his family made me feel as if another healing circle could be completed. It felt as if the dignity that had been taken away during the Nazi time was being restored. Through our connection and shared efforts we were healing the wounds of history that were still present in our families, allowing us to walk in beauty.

Sharing our life experiences and listening to those of others helps us to make sense of our own lives and allows us to create new endings to old stories. In each time I think, "Now I've got it," something always happens to remind me I'm still getting it. I was in Germany again in 2006 at the time of the World Cup Games, the world's greatest sport exhibition. The host country always puts on a colorful display of national pride, and Germany also had a top-contending team. German flags were flying everywhere. Displayed from balconies, stuck on cars, painted on faces, the country was an energized moving tapestry of black, red, and gold.

Expressions of nationalism generally leave me cold, and when I see them in Germany, it's painfully uncomfortable. It takes so little provocation – the raised beer steins, the songs – and I get chills. After World War II, Germans did not make public displays of love for their country. It seemed bad form to express one's German-ness. This year, it was like the Fourth of July. Young people, their faces painted and their Mohawk wigs in the national colors,

sang in the streets by the thousands. Three generations removed from the Nazi era, these young people were standing up to say, "I am proud to be German." After the initial uneasiness, I got caught up in the celebration.

I was in the small town of Freudenstadt, "Happy Town," in the middle of the Black Forest on the afternoon Germany played Argentina in the quarterfinals. Many were gathered in the central square, which was dominated by a huge television screen. When Germany tied the score at the end of regulation play, I stood amidst hundreds of chanting Germans and chanted with them. After a scoreless double-overtime, the game was decided by penalty kicks, and Germany won the shootout. The square erupted in pandemonium as a flag-draped young man slapped me on the shoulder and invited me to dance with him. I didn't hesitate. We linked arms, hopping, stomping, twirling, and danced with abandon. For the first time in my life, I felt at home in my parent's homeland.

There, that old Pueblo Indian medicine man's voice came to me: "If you want to be able to heal, you have to be able to dance, but you also have to be able to hear your own music." On the plaza in Happy Town that afternoon, I danced with a German teenager, and for the first time, felt the chains of my own enslavement drop away. For the first time, I felt comfortable being German, my new ending to an old story.

"If you want to
be able to heal,
you have to be
able to dance,
but you also
have to be able
to hear your
own music."

Chapter 2

Alter Your Consciousness

The best way to look again at what you know is to alter your consciousness; this means finding a way to look at what's familiar from a new perspective. It requires getting into a trance, a state in which you can drift away and open channels into your unconscious mind. There are many ways to do this. Throughout the ages, people have altered their states of consciousness by using meditation, chanting, drumming, dancing, running, listening to stories around the fire, and using mind-altering substances. All visionary experience is the result of seeing beyond ordinary consciousness. It is the province of artists, musicians, scientists, and prophets.

As a species, we tend to defend ourselves from opening channels into these unconscious realms. We are afraid that if we let ourselves explore these magical, intuitive, unencumbered, frightening, exciting, conflicted, and passionate parts of ourselves, we might lose control, become consumed by them, and move to a place beyond reason or return.

"when we open ourselves to our unconscious mind, it helps maintain our lives in balance"

Actually, the opposite is true. When we open ourselves to our unconscious mind, it helps maintain our lives in balance. The brain wants to experience the mystical, and humans are actually hardwired for such experience. Researchers can show us that areas of the brain are activated in trance states. We have monitored the brains of chanting monks, praying nuns, yogis buried alive, and even shamans in drug-induced states. When they are in trance, they all light up a portion of their brains called the Orientation Association Area (OAA). This part of the brain is responsible for telling us where we are in space. Trance states intensify input into this area, which moves you beyond your actual physical boundaries. It's as if you float in another time and space.

Healers, mystics, and artists throughout history have been able to access that part of the brain because all of them respect those powerful unconscious forces that are beyond their control. Anybody can get in touch with it, but you have to train yourself and be willing to awaken yourself into a more lucid state. When you see things from this "otherworldly" perspective, you get to see where the spirit dwells.

It's actually quite important to exercise this part of your brain. Brain scientists tell us that the brain is always changing itself. This is called neuroplasticity. In other words, if you don't use it, you lose it because there is competition for brain space. If you're not using your brain for what it was intended for, it gets taken over for another purpose. The less we use our visionary capacity, the more entrenched our particular way of seeing becomes. This is the paradox of neuroplasticity; the brain can change itself, but constant repetition can prevent other changes from occurring because you keep using the same neural pathways. Your thoughts travel through well-worn brain routes that become deeply rooted. That's why habitual thoughts and actions tend to become self-perpetuating.

For example, as a kid, I learned early on not to ask for what I really wanted because it was selfish. Instead, I learned to give or do for someone else what it is I wanted to receive. And I will still do it. Once, I was at a dinner party where guests sat at tables of eight and were served family-style. The appetizer was Maryland crab cakes, one of my favorite foods in the world. Before the busboy came to clear the plates, I saw one crab cake left and asked if anybody else wanted it. Just my luck, someone said, "Sure, I'll eat it. Did you want it?" My immediate response was, "No, you go ahead." It didn't even cross my mind to say, "Let's share it." Even though I actually did want that crab cake, I heard that well-traveled neural pathway – don't be selfish.

Bad habits can take over our brain maps because every time we repeat the behavior, it claims more control of the brain and prevents the use of that space for establishing new habits. It's best if you can get it right early on, because bad habits always have a competitive advantage. The longer you do it the way you have always done it, the harder it is to change. Like everything else in life, it's use it or lose it. Dr. Norman Doidge, in his remarkably readable book on neuroplasticity, The Brain that Changes Itself, says so beautifully, "…it's hard to learn a new language when you are tyrannized by the mother tongue." The longer you've heard the message in the language you know best, the more difficult it is to unlearn it.

JILL BOLTE TAYLOR

Just as we are hardwired to experience these altered states of consciousness, natural events within our bodies may also cause us to do so as well. For example, you can get into this space by having a stroke. Jill Bolte Taylor was a 37-year-old neuroscientist working at Harvard when she suffered a stroke. At 7:00 A.M. on December 10, 1996, Jill felt a piercing pain behind her left eye from a blood vessel that had just burst. With a PhD in neuroanatomy, she was uniquely qualified to describe what happened within minutes of her brain injury.

First, she lost her balance. Next, her right arm became paralyzed, and she realized she was having a stroke. Instead of panicking, she focused on the feeling that she was disconnecting from her mind and blending with the space around her. In her book, My Stroke of Insight, she described her experience: "My perception of physical boundaries was no longer limited to my skin and hair. I was enfolded in a blanket of tranquil euphoria... at one with the world and all its creatures, part of the magnificent field of shimmering energy... I felt like a genie liberated from its bottle." (Taylor, 2008)

This euphoric nirvana was accompanied by a rapid deterioration of her ability to walk, talk, and recall much of her life. As the left side of her brain, the rational, organized, analytic part, became less functional, the right side picked up the slack. The right brain is the artistic, creative, intuitive, non-judgmental, in-the-moment side that opened her up to feeling this overwhelming sense of peace and oneness with the cosmos.

However, not all people with left-sided brain injuries experience such blissful insightfulness. Some people sink into difficult, moody states and can act out in all kinds of problematic ways. But for Jill Taylor, her stroke recovery meant choosing to live a more spiritual life, which she differentiates from religious life. Religion, she says, is the story that the left brain tells the right brain in order to explain that awesome awareness. The right brain doesn't need to define it; it just melts into the bliss.

"When you embrace the wonder of what we are as living beings, there is a beautiful lightness."

-Jill Bolte Taylor

It took her eight years to fully recover, and she now speaks to audiences all over the world about her experience. She encourages people to exercise their right brains because it promotes a more peaceful consciousness. Jill says she can get into her right brain whenever she wants. If she feels anger rising, she thinks about somebody or something that brings her pleasure. Jill doesn't need to meditate or otherwise prepare herself. Instead, she says all you have to do is believe that you can tame the left-brain mind. She does it by making time for physical and visual passions; she runs, water skis, plays guitar, and makes stained glass. She tells her audiences we all have brains that we can use better.

Jill Bolte Taylor's stroke of insight was the inner peace she experienced, which connected her to her fellow human beings and the planet. She tells people they can stay healthier if they shift their consciousness from their dominant controlling minds, and instead, trust their hearts to open them to a new way of seeing. In Jill's words, "When you embrace the wonder of what we are as living beings, there is a beautiful lightness."

The brain is hardwired for spiritual experiences. We are programmed to move beyond the physical boundaries of time and space, but we tend to subordinate that part of ourselves to our dominant controlling minds. If we allow ourselves to listen to our souls speak, it would open us up to a whole other way of making sense of the world.

But how do we continue to exercise our minds, to open channels into that mystical portion of the brain? We now have the technical ability to illuminate the brain during mystical states of consciousness. In other words, we can watch where the brain lights up when nuns pray, monks chant, yogis breathe, and dervishes dance.

Altered consciousness is a trance state, and you can get into it by singing, drumming, running, meditating, visualizing, and sitting in awe. Since humankind began, the species has found ways to kindle this altered state of consciousness. In order to grow, to be creative, there must be a willingness to unlearn the familiar and open paths into the less-used portions of your neuroplastic brain. By firing different neurons, you kindle another state of consciousness.

You can also get into a trance state through active imagination. Anatoly Sharansky, the Soviet human rights activist, spent nine years in prison. Of those nine years, 400 days of the sentence was spent in solitary confinement in a freezing, dark, 5-foot-by-6-foot punishment cell. Political prisoners in isolation often fall apart mentally because of the use-it-or-lose-it principle. The brain needs external stimulation to maintain its maps. During this extended period of sensory deprivation, Sharansky played mental chess. He played it for months on end without a chessboard or the pieces. Sharansky imagined them and kept track of all the positions. He played both white and black, holding the game in his head from opposite perspectives, which is an extraordinary challenge to the brain

When Sharansky was released, he emigrated to Israel and ultimately became a cabinet minister. When Chess Grandmaster Garry Kasparov came to Israel, he played against the prime minister and leaders of the cabinet. Kasparov was able to beat them all, except for Sharansky. Once you develop the capacity to see in new ways, it never leaves you.

Just as chess opened Sharansky's mind, you can get into a trance state through the use of mind-altering drugs. There's been an increase of research done on the use of mind-altering drugs in the treatment of addictions and post-traumatic stress disorders. Until recently, most of these studies have been conducted outside the United States. Groundbreaking studies have also been conducted in the treatment of opiate addiction using LSD and Ibogaine. Ibogaine has pharmacologic components that relieve the symptoms of opiate withdrawal, its impact demonstrable and long-lasting. Researchers are now experimenting with the use of MDMA (Ecstasy), marijuana, and hallucinogens in the treatment of Post-Traumatic Stress Disorder, Obsessive Compulsive Disorder, and depression. Initial results have been quite favorable. These drugs, however, cannot yet be legally prescribed.

Ketamine is a drug with hallucinogenic properties and the only one that can be legally prescribed. It's primarily used as a pre-anesthetic by physicians, dentists, and veterinarians, but it does have a side effect that some people don't enjoy. Ketamine has short acting psychedelic characteristics. In other words, it induces a dissociative state that causes people to lose track of time and place and to detach from an awareness of external stimuli, including pain. I have used it in my own clinical practice in treating Steve, a 64-year-old attorney with metastatic liver cancer suffering from depression and end-of-life anxiety.

In his fifties, Steve was diagnosed with non-alcoholic cirrhosis. Ten years later, he was diagnosed with liver cancer that by then had begun to spread. By the time I met Steve, the cancer had spread to his lungs, and he was no longer eligible for liver transplant. Steve wanted me to find him a Native American medicine man to perform a peyote ceremony for him and alter his consciousness. He was quite specific; he wanted to go back to the lost continent of Atlantis.

I wondered at first if perhaps his cancer had spread to his brain and he had become delusional.

DR. H AMD STEVE

But he was rational, bright, articulate, quick-witted, and insightful, and I liked him. We had plenty in common. We were both graduates of New York City public high schools and colleges. He was Jewish in the ethnic sense – he liked pastrami and matzoh-ball soup – but he did not believe in a personal God.

Steve had gone on to law school and ultimately become a federal judge. He had been divorced for many years, had two grown, independent and successful children and a live-in girlfriend.

He was angry with the doctors who had missed his spreading disease and were now saying it was too late to treat him. Steve was not ready to die. Instead, he wanted to go back in time to speak to the Atlantean shaman who held the power to heal him. I told him even if we could find such a medicine man, eating the peyote cactus makes the gut go into an uproar. Vomiting is common, and he had already bled from his gut. But there were other options, I said, and we talked about the many ways there were to alter consciousness.

First, I hypnotized him. Steve was able to regress if not to Atlantis, at least to a Neanderthal cave. He approached the cave entrance and saw the cavemen around the fire but did not enter.

Steve asked if there was anything else that might help him go deeper. We talked about many consciousness-altering drugs, from marijuana to entheogens (hallucinogens). I told him about Ketamine, a controlled substance that induces a dissociative state where you lose track of time and detach from the awareness of external stimuli. Anesthe-

siologists and veterinarians have used it as a pre-anesthetic, and psychiatrists are researching it for use with addictions and PTSD. I told Steve that although I knew about Ketamine therapy, I'd never used it in my clinical practice before, but if he were interested, I would consider it as long as it was also okay with his family.

I gave him literature to review and told him to discuss it with his children, one of whom was a physician. When he returned, he'd done his homework and wanted to try it. He had experimented with LSD in the '60s and wasn't frightened by the experience. He knew I'd be with him and totally involved. I spoke with his children who not only supported his decision, but also added that it didn't surprise them at all.

Steve brought along some crystals and stones that he had collected from Mayan sites in the Yucatán to the first session. He said they reminded him of ancient wisdom. I told him to spread them around wherever he wanted and then lit the candle and some cedar incense on the coffee table between us. I prepared the space and spoke of my wish for him to see and hear things to help him find what he needed to know. Then I gave him a cautious, low dose to see his tolerance, and within three minutes, he described a warm tingling in his ears that spread to his face and lips. Then he had an overwhelming sense of peace and well-being. "The world is so beautiful," he said and described the experience as "an endless orgasm."

In his altered state, Steve went back to the Neanderthal cave, and this time they made room for him around the fire even though he couldn't understand a word they were saying. He looked around and saw beautiful artwork on the cave walls. The handprints reached out to him, and he got up to touch them. Watching him, the Neanderthal shaman came over and put his hand next to Steve's on the cave wall and then outlined them both by spitting a chalky fluid over both their hands. He knew he had met his shaman but had no idea what he was saying to him.

Steve wanted to learn more, and I doubled the dose at the next visit. The same enveloping warmth and peace came over him. He heard the music and started humming, and I joined him. Then his hands started moving over his body, and I put my hands over his and followed along. He said it spread the healing light all over his body. He pressed his hands deeply into his liver, and I pressed mine in too. After that session, he started feeling better and started going back to his health club. A month later, I increased the dose again. After the celestial chorus started humming, tears rolled down his cheeks, and he said, "I have never felt so connected to the whole universe."

Despite feeling better, routine blood work revealed rising tumor markers. Steve found a research program at the University of Pittsburgh that would accept him and inject drugs directly into the liver. However, he had to discontinue his Ketamine therapy because they didn't know how it might interfere with their medicines.

For the next several months, he flew to Pittsburgh, but when his tumor markers were only getting higher, they said they were going to stop the treatment. When he got home, he was seriously depressed and asked for another Ketamine session. What he was seeking now was less a demand for a cure than it was a wish for discovery.

Minutes after injecting the drug, the humming began and morphed into a traditional Hebrew chant. Steve saw the prophet Abraham in a flowing white gown standing above his son Isaac, who was lying in front of him. As he got closer, he saw that the flowing robe was actually a doctor's white coat and that he was Isaac, bound to a hospital stretcher. When he heard God's voice command Dr. Abraham, "Do not kill the boy," Steve began to cry. Only later did he tell me that he finally understood what the Neanderthal shaman was telling him at the cave wall. "I saw my body lying on that altar, and when I heard the voice of God say 'Do not kill the boy,' I saw the dagger in Abraham's hand turn into a light, which illuminated the darkness above me," said Steve. "Then I saw his hand become my handprint on the cave wall."

Steve understood that the body gets taken. What is most important is the imprint he leaves behind. Steve died two months later, comfortable and at peace, more than ten years after his original diagnosis and five times longer than anyone had predicted he would live.

Steve's work with Ketamine allowed him to live and die in the pursuit of his true self. It was not God for whom he reached at the end of life; he was a lawyer who sought more evidence before resting his case. Instead, through an altered state of consciousness, Steve discovered that if you let go of your automatic self and lose control of the ordinary ways of seeing, you may move from struggle to transformation. Steve was never cured, but he was healed. Healing is facing the truth of who you are and seeing beyond your limitations. You can still be healed even if you're not cured. Healing, rather, is a psycho-spiritual condition.

Every individual, tribe, and culture has perfectly logical explanations that account for the mysterious universe. Every tribe has its own stories about why we are born the unique souls we are, why tragedy befalls us, and why miracles happen. You don't have to be dying to seek a teacher who can help you see the world from this perspective. You don't have to get to a place where staying alive is always foremost on your mind. You have to find a place where those thoughts take a backseat so that you can live in the moment. You can open yourself to that place where the spirit soars and explore the edge of the unknown because that's where we dare to imagine what else is out there.

> "Healing is facing the truth of who you are and seeing beyond your limitations."

The work in psychedelic therapy is growing rapidly, and researchers are reporting that patients and control groups who were exposed to only a single dose felt better after the experience. People say it often produces one of the most spiritually significant experiences they'd ever had. If we can explore these states in a guided experience with people we trust, it can help people live fuller, richer lives with the time they have left.

One of my most spiritually significant experiences occurred on a recent clown trip to Peru with my friend and holy brother, Patch Adams, M.D., the world's most recognized humanitarian clown. While in the jungle, I had the opportunity to do something that's been on my bucket list for a long time. I wanted to explore the Amazon beyond the river towns, to go upriver into the jungle to hear it, feel it, and participate with an authentic shaman in an ayahuasca ceremony.

I arranged for a two-day trip up into the headwaters of the Amazon in a dugout canoe. I went with five friends, all fellow clowns, up the Yarapa River into Cocama Indian Country. On the way, we were treated to the sounds and sights of the jungle – egrets, herons, kingfisher, fish eagles, toucans, a million butterflies, huge flying insects, pink river dolphins, turtles, and fishermen netting Piranhas. It was magical.

We got to the lodge, an elevated wooden shack, where the ceremony would be held and met the ayahuasquero, the shaman. Really named Don Juan, the 67-year-old Cocama Indian is descended from generations of shamans. No more than 5 feet 6 inches tall, the vigorous, smiling, and engaging Don Juan invited us to his farm. He wanted to show us how the sacred ayahuasca vine grew and was prepared. We piled back into the dugout canoe to meet his family and walk the fields. He showed us many therapeutic plants, plenty of bugs and frogs, and at the sacred vine, he lit a cigarette to bless it and us. Don Juan asked if any of us had ever taken

DON JUAN

ayahuasca before – one of us had – and he summarized what the experience might be like. We might get sick to our stomachs, but he advised us to sit up and let it out. "Only then can you see something new," he said.

Aya/huasca, which means "devil/vine" in Quechua, cleanses the body by unleashing a parasympathetic cascade that induces vomiting and can cause diarrhea. You sweat profusely and can become immobilized. Don Juan said one first had to let go of the stuff that's trapped inside in order to make room to see things more clearly.

It is the Chakruna leaf that is added to the Mariri vine that makes the ayahuasca, the sacramental tea that induces the visions. I had hoped I might see deeper into the mind's mystery. It was completely dark when we began. A half-hour before, I could hear the shaman vomiting outside. Don Juan took the ayahuasca mixture before we did to prepare himself, and that was the first time I felt a queasiness telling me that I may be in for a little more than a sick stomach.

We gathered in a 10-foot-by-20-foot shack containing six mosquito-netted beds, one toilet, and a sink. We sat in a small circle on the floor. In the cen-ter sat a burning candle. Don Juan lit a cigarette and blew the smoke over a large jar that contained the vile, syrupy mixture. He filled a juice glass, a little less for the women, and passed it to each of us in succession. When we were done drinking it, he picked up a fan, also called a shakapa, made of branches with tiny leaves and waved out the flame. Don Juan began to whistle a tune that

DON JUAN AND DR. H.

mixed with the sounds of the jungle night. It was an entrancing lullaby and made me think about my mother around the Sabbath lights.

After thirty minutes, I was feeling a bit woozy, and the sounds got a little blurry. In another ten minutes, the first round of nausea seized me. I got really sick — no orifice remained inactive — and my legs trembled so that I could hardly stand. I was sweating profusely and was quite thirsty, so I asked for water. A helper brought me a glass, but Don Juan told me not to drink it, so I dutifully put it down next to me. But after another twenty minutes of continued fluid loss, I was even more lightheaded, so I asked for water again. However, Don Juan told me not to drink because it would only make me sicker.

At that point, I was thinking, "I'm a doctor; he's a jungle shaman. I'm fluid depleted, my circulating volume is down, my heart, lungs and brain are stressing out. I need water. It's pitch black, and he can't see me, so I'll just pick up the glass." I reached over to where I had put down the glass, but it wasn't

Alter Your Consciousness

there. "Water," I moaned, and without a response, it was finally clear to me that I was in his jungle. I understood that he knew something I needed to learn and to trust the process.

After that, it wasn't fifteen minutes before the vomiting stopped, and then I lay down. Animals came walking by, generally two-by-two, but sometimes families as well. I could speak to them all, but by morning, I couldn't recall a single conversation. There were no surrounding celestial lights or heavenly throne. Instead, my great vision had been how hard it was to let go and trust that someone or something other than myself could get me through the night.

These mind-altering substances have been critical to my objective learning process in becoming more human. I could live without these tune-ups but choose not to. They remind me that I am blessed to be a part of this life, that I am truly a living, breathing, working part of this universe with the power to choose how to evolve consciously.

"When you are ready to hear the story, you can create a new ending."

Every time I reacquaint myself with this power, it awakens my spirit to its renewal. It's still clear to me that I prefer having the paddle to my canoe in my own hands, but I have learned to tame my ego sufficiently, to place myself in someone else's hands so that I don't have to retch in agony in my jungle of preconceptions before I give up the control I never had anyway. Even in elderhood, you can see the familiar in a new way and let go the old, rutted pathways that keep you chained to old behaviors. When you are ready to hear the story, you can create a new ending.

Chapter 3

Everything Is Filled With Spirit

Do you remember your childhood teddy bear? The one that kept you company when things got rough, who showed you how to love and take care of yourself when you faced the night alone? Everything that holds good memories for us contains a feeling, an essence inspiring us when life seems impossible. Bears, baseballs, rosary beads, stones, sea shells, crystals, wooden carvings, your mother's chicken soup, even the smell of chocolate chip cookies in the oven are filled with an energy that helps us through the hard times. They are reminders of loving connections and help us when we face new life challenges like a move, job loss, new boss, divorce, or disease. Then those reminders become energetically-invested, sacred objects. They have an energy that inspires the soul.

"Everything that holds good memories for us contains a feeling, an essence inspiring us when life seems impossible."

Everything that exists in the universe, every stone, animal, and tree, can be seen in a new way. They all contain their own energies, which we often overlook. Every scientific discipline and religious group describes that energy in its own words. Physicists tell us that this energy is carried in particles and flows in waves, and that energy and matter are interchangeable.

Priests and shaman call that energetic principal "God" or the "Great Spirit." Physicists, priests, and shamans all believe there is an underlying causal process that explains the harmony of the universe hidden from ordinary view. It doesn't matter how we define this energy. It matters more that we acknowledge it exists.

Indigenous healers know that everything in the universe contains this unfathomable energy that they call "Spirit," or Wakan, Hozho, Mastamho, Chi. They see the energy in all things, and by careful observation, the shamans find ways to tap into those energies. Shamans have found how to establish concrete connections with everything in their environment. They learn to befriend stones, plants, animals, clouds, and ancestors. They learn their secrets and then use them to promote healing. Shamans spend years developing relationships with these friends whom they call their spiritual allies. These allies accompany shamans everywhere. They call upon them if they need help making diagnoses, identifying the lost parts that must be restored if a patient is to become whole again.

These allies inspire the healer and the patient to believe that they will help make the difference in bringing the patient back to wellness. This energetic connection with their allies, who may speak in strange languages and appear in visions, always teaches them something they would otherwise never have seen.

If this sounds a bit metaphysical, let me assure you this is also the language of science. Doctors ally themselves to their machines and technology but their healing story could be told this way:

> *The medicine man enters the outer vestibule of the sacred healing chamber. He dons the ceremonial vestments and performs the ritual motions, purifying himself for the healing ritual that is about to begin. Putting on identical masks, the medicine man and his acolytes enter the chamber to which all others are forbidden entrance. The patient has already been ushered into a deep trance by another shaman using a magical elixir. Within the chamber, the ritual instruments have been purified, and only the initiated are allowed to touch them. The shaman calls for each implement in turn, handed to him by an acolyte. He uses these in a ritual scarification procedure that removes a small part of the ill man's body. When he awakens from the trance, the patient is magically healed, though some further ceremonies are required before he is able to leave the grounds of the Temple of Healing." (Eisenstein, C., The Ascent of Humanity, 2009).*

All healers go through many years of training, which includes tests, initiation ordeals, and the mastery of an esoteric language. Upon completing training, they become agents of the healing transformation. Western-trained physicians too often depend solely on their technology to become agents of the healing transformation while dramatically underutilizing symbolic instruments and ceremonies that could intensify their healing power. I am a Western-trained physician who believes in evidence-based medicine, but I've also expanded my definition of what evidence is because I've seen the

healing power of symbols, rituals, and ceremonies. I have incorporated songs, aromas, stories, and trances into my therapeutic repertoire, which has intensified my power as a healer. I even create healing ceremonies.

Along with colleagues from the Turtle Island Project (www.turtleislandproject.com), I recently conducted an experiential workshop entitled "Creating Healing Ceremonies." The project was founded by Western and Native Amer-

Turtle Island Project Board with Mona Polacca, the Hopi representative of the 13 Indigenous Grandmothers (in front, dressed in red and white)

ican healers interested in learning from each other and integrating each other's stories, symbols, rituals, and ceremonies into their healing practices. Ceremonies, for example, provide the structure by which people get in touch with their feelings, and that's where the human spirit dwells. If you can inspire that soulful place, you can stimulate the healing process.

As a preparation for the workshop, participants were asked to bring along a sacred object, not necessarily a religious one, but something that held special significance for them. During the workshop, we explored ways to intensify the power of their sacred or symbolic objects. Using the language of neuroscience as well as legends, dance, drums, meditation, and ceremonies, we explored many ways to influence healing.

One of the attendees was participating for her second time. Brenda had completed a year-long treatment program for a metastatic cancer just three weeks before this workshop and wanted to celebrate the end of a torturous regimen of surgery, radiation, and chemotherapy. She was declared cancer-free and left mostly hairless, without saliva or taste, and easily tired. Brenda felt like a deeply scarred warrior and wanted to welcome her future.

We set the stage for Brenda's healing ceremony by telling the story of the Native American Sun Dance ceremony. Among the tribes of the Great Plains, this ceremony ensures their survival as tribe and the planet. In this annual summer ritual, warriors pierce their flesh and hang from a tree until they break free to fulfill their vows to themselves, their ancestors, and the earth mother.

In Brenda's ceremony, we would sing and dance to those songs, while as a group, we created a healing mask for her. She lay down on a long table clutching her sacred object to her chest. A Hopi/Havasupai medicine woman blessed the space and prepared Brenda's face. I applied a plaster cast to her face, leaving her eyes uncovered.

While the mask was drying, the other participants, holding their sacred objects, circled the table to the drum beat and songs. Everyone had an opportunity to look directly into Brenda's eyes. They touched her, whispered to her, and filled her mask with the healing power of their love and investment in her continued health.

I knew the impact of the ceremony of myself and those who participated, but I wondered how Brenda would remember the ceremony and how it would impact her life. This is Brenda's story:

Everything is Filled With Spirit

I learned about healing in community at last year's retreat, "The Last Mask Of The Authentic Healer." It was in this workshop that Claudia formed a plaster mask around my face three days before I was to learn that I had Stage IV cancer in my sinus cavity that had metastasized into my brain and bi-laterally in my neck. This mask captured the large tumors in my neck, and oddly enough, I decorated the mask in a way that looked sickly.

Grandmother Mona drummed with her brothers and sisters at this retreat and sang healing native songs. Dr. H. told healing stories, sang native songs, and played the water drum that he had so eloquently put together. The music, stories, and people all made this retreat sing to my soul. Grandmother Mona put her hands on my neck, gazed into my eyes with a peace I had never known, and said a prayer for me. Dr. H. and Mona taught us about the how healing is possible through rituals. This retreat transformed my life and gave me a new way to look at the people who crossed my path. I came to the realization that I am never alone as long as I see all of humanity as my brothers and sisters.

This new way of seeing would later be the key to my successful healing. The native music and drumming, followed by Grandmother Mona putting her hands on my neck and saying a prayer, was instrumental in my healing. I listened to native songs as a source of comfort during my treatment and saw Grandmother Mona's face with her peaceful eyes in my visions. The love and support that my partner and I received during treatment was amazing, and the depth of support restored my faith in humanity. I have never known this depth of love and support, and I commend all of those who supported us through this trying time.

I endured thirteen months of rigorous cancer treatment, including surgeries, chemotherapies, and radiation. When Dr. H. announced this year's retreat, "Healing Ceremonies," I knew that I would only be three weeks out of chemotherapy and final treatment, but the timing seemed to be serendipitous. I wanted to celebrate the end of my treatment and my new way of seeing with the "Healing Ceremonies" retreat. I had no idea how much I could do and decided that I would do the best that I could and rest when I needed to rest. This retreat was equally transforming.

Dr. H. asked if I would be willing to participate in a group healing ceremony where he would make a healing mask for me. I can't explain the emotions that rushed through my body. I felt honored, scared, and totally excited all at one time. The tears flowed from my eyes, and I had no idea what this would all mean to me. I was in total awe over the anticipation of this experience.

Before my healing ceremony, Dr. H. randomly selected three small groups and asked us to create a healing ceremony for one of the group members. I learned how to create a healing ceremony for one of my sisters and saw the impact of healing ceremonies. Through these healing ceremonies, I was drawn closer to the entire group and especially to my individual team. It is uncanny how the selected groups became a perfect match for all of us. It also gave me an idea of what the healing ceremony for me might look like that evening.

The ceremony was to start after dinner, so I had some time to lie down and pray for the ability to stay present and take in all that was about to happen with a heart of gratitude. When I entered the group room, I saw a long thin conference table set up in the middle of the room with towels covering it. There was a folded towel on the end of the table that led me to believe that I would be lying down on this table. I had to catch my breath at the initial sight and walked out back to look at the stars and pray once again to stay present with an open heart. I asked the Great Spirit to bless me and the group in white light and allow me to feel the healing that was about to take place.

I lay down on the table and again prayed for the white light and healing. Dr. H. told me that Claudia cut up the strips of plaster to make my healing mask. Grandmother Mona, whose healing hands have touched many people all over this world, would apply the Vaseline to my face. He would then create the healing mask that the entire group would later decorate. The lights were subdued and the mood was created.

Grandmother Mona's hands gently and ritualistically touched my face as she deliberately applied the Vaseline. She told me that she was honored to be doing this for me, but it was I who felt honored to be receiving her gift. I continued to breathe in the healing touch, and then Dr. H. began to apply the plaster strips to create this healing mask. He told me that he would leave the eye holes open so that every group member could dance around the table and show me their sacred objects as they moved. He would sing the Lakota Sundance song, which represents a song for warriors. The honor, gratitude, and excitement were overwhelming.

I closed my eyes as the mask was being made. The water from the plaster strips dripped into my eyes, onto my ears and neck, and to back of my head. I can still feel the healing waters on my skin. This mask was created with detail and balance. I had the vision of the sickly mask that Claudia created for me last year and felt an excitement about my new mask and new life cancer free. I thought about the rigorous treatment over the past year and how I learned

DR. HAMMERSCHLAG WITH BRENDA

Everything is Filled With Spirit

about a will to live through the toughest time of my life. The entire year had been about transforming from being sick to being healed, and this mask represented all that I was about to become.

The mask was done, and Dr. H. wiped the water from my eyes. He held my hand, and the drumming and singing started as the entire group danced around me on the table. I saw the group, their sacred objects, and felt their hearts through their eyes and touch. They held my hand, touched my feet, and said prayers over my head. I couldn't help but smile. The mask shaded me enough that I was able to see deeply and feel the healing. People leaned over the table to look at me through my mask with the most loving eyes I had ever seen. I could see and be seen like never before. These objects danced, people danced, and I completely felt the love. My heart was touched so deeply as I thought to myself, "They are all doing this for me." This is the love that I felt during my treatment, and it is a love that could only come from the Great Spirit. It is the true essence of healing.

Dr. H. removed the mask from my face, and I could see the group with a different set of eyes. I hugged every group member and felt like I knew their hearts on a deeper level. Tears fell from my eyes with a feeling of honor, love, gratitude, and awe. No words can describe this experience, and Dr. H. knew it. He said to go back to our rooms and hold the experience in our hearts without talking about it. Something absolutely incredible had happened, and we all knew it.

I went back to my room and took a shower to get all of the plaster off me. There were no words to describe what I had just experienced, and as the water sprayed on my bald head, I started to weep. What greater gift could I receive than the gift of healing? The only word I could come up with to describe what just happened was, "awe." Describing it now seems so limiting in comparison to what I actually experienced.

We had an early morning sweat the next day. This was the longest period of time that I had been up in a given day without taking a nap. I approached the sweat with a sense of cleansing from so many chemotherapy and radiation treatments. The sweat was beautiful, and I could feel the toxins drip out of my body. Again the songs, prayers, and community solidified my experience from the night before. I could feel the heat on my radiated neck and face. I took a buff into the sweat and covered myself when necessary. I witnessed the power of ceremony, and Grandmother Mona led the most beautiful sweat with graciousness in prayer and song. I

"…it is through sharing the story that others will know the power of healing. I still don't know that the story will give the experience the power that it deserves, but I know that I am truly blessed."

-Brenda

heard the cries of pain and quest for healing during this sweat and couldn't think of any other place that I wanted to be.

During the brunch period, the group was encouraged to decorate my healing mask. Before entering the group room, Gloria walked out and told me that this mask was different than she expected it to be. She walked me into the room, and I saw people cutting locks of hair to give my mask the hair that I didn't have on my head. One man was bald so he cut his chest hair. They didn't have scissors, so they used a knife to cut their hair so that I could have some. One woman told me that when Grandmother Mona put sage and cedar on the ancient's lava rocks during the sweat, she swore that she saw a butterfly. She said that she was inspired to color a butterfly on my mask as a result of this vision. It is the most beautiful mask and punctuated a new beginning for me.

I brought the mask home and set it next to last year's mask. The difference between the two masks is enormous. Last year's mask is decorated in dark colors with a large neck amplifying the tumors. The new mask has bright colors, hair, and a smile. I can still hear the beautiful voices and feel the gentle healing touch. I can see the people and sacred objects dancing around me, and I feel so alive. I asked Dr. H. how to explain this to others and give it the power that it deserves, and he told me that it is through sharing the story that others will know the power of healing. I still don't know that the story will give the experience the power that it deserves, but I know that I am truly blessed.

Just as Brenda experienced the healing power of ritual and its sense of spiritual enlightenment, I had a similar awakening. I've had back pain for most of my adult life and three surgical procedures to repair herniated discs between the ages of 36 and 45. The surgeries left me with significant postoperative complications. I was healed by a Hopi Indian medicine man who was my friend and spiritual guide, a story that I share in The Dancing Healers. Herbert took a six-hour bus ride to come and see me right in the middle of his planting season, because after the failure of his first corn planting, he had a dream in which I was featured.

In the dream, his cornfield was barren except for a single, withered stalk atop which was a single ear. As he approached the stalk and looked closely at it, the ear of corn had my face. My mouth was open and pleading, but he could not hear the words. He came closer but still couldn't hear because my mouth was open but speaking soundlessly.

Herbert came to see me because he understood that there was something going on in my life that had influenced his planting and was threatening me. He wanted to know what was going on in my life. The dream disquieted me to say the least, but at the moment, I couldn't think of anything special going on in my life. Herbert sat silently, and then I remembered I was planning to go to the Mayo Clinic in Rochester Minnesota for my fourth operation.

Herbert looked at me and said I should not have the operation. As much as I valued his opinion, I was still a believer in the edifice of surgical science to restore me to health. I had found the best surgeon and picked the finest facility. "Why should I not have surgery?" I asked him. Herbert responded that this is what the dream was about. I was that lean, dying corn stalk with the big head and open mouth that wasn't saying anything. My mouth could not speak because I was not standing in truth. Herbert said my stalk was telling me something my head did not want to know, and it was killing me.

It still wasn't clear to me until he told me to pay more attention to what my body was telling me rather than what my mind was telling me to do. Only then did it come to me that my bullshit was killing me. If I continued to believe my manhood would crumble if I gave up competitive athletics, then I was going to keep aggravating my back pain. My wish for surgical relief was a way to avoid facing my whole truth and changing my lifestyle.

I went to the Mayo Clinic anyway, and a renowned back surgeon told me that even with surgery, I had only a 50/50 chance of operative success. He added that if I made some lifestyle changes and stopped playing competitive racquetball and basketball and did some lower impact exercises like swimming, he thought I could live reasonably pain-free.

This time I heard Herbert's dream clearly — get it straight, change your way of seeing, look again at what you know, and face your truth today. It would have been easier if I could only have heard that wisdom earlier in my life. Alas, we are always limited by what we can see in any moment. If we are open to expanding our energetic resources, such as dreams, plants, animals, and healers, then we magnify our power to heal.

The recent book and movie, *The Horse Boy*, is a glowing example of an energetic connection between an autistic boy and a horse. When Rowan Isaacson was 2 years old, he was diagnosed with autism. He manifested all the classical symptoms. He stopped talking, retreated into himself, avoided eye contact, and screamed uncontrollably. His father, Rupert, noticed that when Rowan wandered into a neighbor's horse pasture, a testy quarter horse dipped her head in a submissive posture and stood perfectly still. When the horse calmed down, so did the boy. Rupert, an avid horseman, was intrigued and took his son for a horseback ride. Holding the boy in front of him, they walked and then trotted. Rowan became quiet and uttered his first new word in a year. As they continued to ride together, his tantrums and isolationism lessened.

Rupert, a journalist who had written about what he experienced with Kalahari Bushmen, looked for an indigenous culture that combined horsemanship with shamanic healing. He discovered the oldest horseman tribes that still practiced shamanism were the Durkha in Outer Mongolia. Rupert took his wife, Kristin, and his son to participate in these healing ceremonies. The boy was exposed to an assortment of rituals that included animals and ordeals. When it was over, Rowan's emotional fire-storms stopped, he talked more, and by the time they returned to the States, he was potty trained for the first time.

So how does one explain this? Was it the ceremonies, the animals, or the new relationships? The result does not lend itself to an easy explanation, because the power of reason is limited in explaining the universe. It's clear, however, that some new pathway of learning opened Rowan to seeing what was familiar from another perspective.

"The magic of all therapy is in finding ways to open new channels into the mind that allow one to move beyond old limitations."

The worlds of autism and shamanism intersected. Both the shaman and the boy found a way to go into their own worlds, worlds where they connected with their demons and allies. Rowan looked at the shaman, watched him go into trance, and then saw how he came out of it and reconnected with the world. The magic of all therapy is in finding ways to open new channels into the mind that allow one to move beyond old limitations.

Equine-assisted therapy is an increasingly popular treatment modality for people living with various physical and emotional challenges, including autism. There is a physical stimulation when riding that exercises the same pelvic and trunk muscles used for walking, and it also improves balance and coordina-tion. Sitting high up on the horse can do wonders for the rider's confidence, and then there is the energetic relationship be-tween horse and rider. The horse knows when the rider tenses, and as their trust and experience grows, they move together with greater confidence. There is something about the con-nection between Rowan and horses that allowed him to reach a place inside himself that moved him beyond his old path of symptomatic isolation.

There are also modern shamans who utilize these principles in downtown Taipei. Chang Yin, a jitong or Chinese shaman, sees patients in a busy mod-ern office building, as described in an article from The New York Times in December, 2008. She is carrying on the folk tradition that goes back to an-tiquity. Ms. Chang dispenses advice while channeling a spirit that comes to her in a trance. In the past, such shamans played a central role in village life. Based in local temples, they settled disputes, dispensed counsel, and healed the sick by channeling spirits.

In today's developing economies of modern cities, people still come to the ji-

Everything is Filled With Spirit

tong. The questions they ask may be a little different because the community and workplace have changed, but they still come to seek guidance about marital problems, raising children, and family conflicts. Ms. Chang has adapted this shamanic tradition to meet the needs of modern city dwellers. She regularly sends text messages to about 300 clients and has created a virtual community network that has replaced the old, tightly-knit village.

Ms. Chang does not charge for her shamanic healing services; most of her income comes from teaching and advising businesses on feng shui. In an interview, she said that she was called to be a jitong. She did not choose it. When she was six years old, she asked her mother why there were people walking in the sky through the clouds. Ms. Chang said her parents didn't blame her or think that she was making it up. Instead, they brought her a book with pictures of holy beings and asked her which one she had seen.

When she was 12, a Buddhist priest began teaching her the ways of the jitong. At 16, she was capable of being possessed by the spirit of Ji Gong, a maverick Chinese-Buddhist monk who lived in the twelfth century. After completing school, she held several jobs but said the spirits kept pestering her to be a jitong and to deliver their messages.

Ms. Chang said that along with changes in society, the jitongs needed to adjust their practices. People still needed advice, guidance, support, and hope from a believable person who was experienced in mobilizing healing energies.

Professor Ting Jen-chieh, a specialist in Taiwanese religion at the Institute of Technology of the Academia Sinica in Taipei, said, "Although we have become middle-class oriented, 70% of Taiwanese still adhere to some traditional ways. We believe the jitong channels the spirits of revered ancestors, so when they speak, we pay attention to what they're saying."

Shamanic healers have existed in every culture. They are wise, experienced, skillful, well-respected people who help us through hard times.

I first learned about the International Council of 13 Indigenous Grandmothers from Mona Polacca, my beloved sister, who is one of them. Five years ago, 13 grandmothers, their ages ranging from their fifties to their eighties and representing indigenous people in the Americas, Asia, and Africa, came together to share a vision for the healing of the planet and its peoples. They connected as a collective to speak for the Earth mother and to keep this a sacred home for humanity. They were com-

THIRTEEN INDIGENOUS GRANDMOTHERS

mitted to building a global community through their praying, peacemaking, and healing work. They wished to maintain their ceremonial practices, affirm the right to use plant medicines free of legal restrictions, and protect the land where indigenous people lived and upon which their cultures depended. Since their coming together as the International Council of 13 Indigenous Grandmothers in 2004, the Grandmothers have been the subject of a book and movie, have spoken at the United Nations, and have met with the Dalai Lama and the Pope.

Mona and I first worked together in the early '70s when she worked as a mental health specialist for the Colorado River Indian Tribes in Arizona. She is Hopi, Tewa, and Havasupai, holds a Masters of Social Work (MSW) degree, and is a social worker, spiritual leader, and healer. We are both among the

co-founders of the Turtle Island Project, a non-profit foundation that conducts retreats and workshops to teach the incorporation of Native American healing rituals within western medicine. Mona says, "I pray for people. That's all I do. I acknowledge my ancestors and all those who came before who made it possible for us to be here today." Mona says that prayers are like an arrowhead that moves in front of her making a way, clearing a path, and all she does is walk behind it. She travels around the world telling her story about how we can utilize all resources around us to build a foundation that will carry our youth healthily into the future.

DR. H., MONA, AND MASK-MAKER CLAUDIA WEINSPACH OF THE TURTLE ISLAND PROJECT FACULTY

Mona is among a handful of people who have taught me how to pray. Prayer is a song that comes from your heart to your lips without thinking about it first. Speech is something that comes from the head to the lips after considering its potential impact or reception. To speak directly from the heart to the lips without thinking about it is a prayer. The more we come from a prayerful place, the more ways we find to connect to our universe.

Every year, one of the 13 Indigenous Grandmothers brings all the others to visit her tribe. When it was Mona's turn to bring the Grandmothers to Phoenix in 2009, she introduced the Turtle Island Project board members to her sisters. This is where I met Aama Bombo, also known as Buddhi Maya Lama, a Tamang from Nepal. Her father was a renowned shaman, but in her tribe, women were not permitted to practice traditional healing, and her father restricted the development of her visionary gifts.

Everything is Filled With Spirit

When she was 25, Aama developed violent shaking all over her body, which lasted for over a year. The people around her thought she had become mentally ill and took her to see many healers for a cure but to no avail. Before she was to be admitted to a psychiatric hospital, Aama's grandmother took her to a Buddhist lama who told her what was the matter with her. In the nine years since her father's death, his spirit had been seeking someone through whom he could transmit his teachings. But he could not find anyone with a good enough heart. He had to accept that even though she was female, she was the one through to which he could transmit his teachings. The shaking was her father reaching out to her. As soon as she was able to recognize his spirit within her and that of others, she stopped shaking.

AAMA BOMBO (BUDDHI MAYA LAMA)

Grandmother Aama is a well-known shaman in Nepal who treats the poorest of the poor as well as members of the royal family. People arrive at her home by 6:00 A.M., and the healing goes on until noon. After a short rest, she resumes her work. She can easily see one hundred people a day. She guides them on the journey during which she helps them find an untapped power that lies within them. Grandmother Aama channels a host of spirits. First, she calls on her father's spirit, then the spirits of her clan and the nature spirits that surround her. Finally, she calls the spirit of the powerful Hindu deity, Hanuman, who delivers man from the forces of evil. She channels all these spirits and deities, and through her work, she has become a trusted go-between for the long-standing political divisions in Nepal.

BERNADETTE REBIENOT

Another of the Grandmothers, Bernadette Rebienot, is Omyene and from Gabon. Bernadette's own grandmother was an initiated shaman who was taught the traditional healing practices from Gabon's rain forest Pygmies. Through her, Bernadette was introduced to the plants of the ancestors that needed to be protected for future generations. She listened to the stories of how to respect the forest and to speak for the Mother.

Bernadette was about to start school when her mother died. Nuns in a convent school then raised her until she became seriously ill. The right side of her face became paralyzed in excruciating pain. Sunlight intensified her illness, and she was forced to stay in darkness. The illness lasted three years despite the efforts of modern medicine. Her grandmother brought Bernadette to see her Pygmy master, who told her that she had a special gift and that she had to accept the illness as her path to initiation. It was he who initiated her into the sacred medicine, Iboga.

When the Iboga root is chewed, a person can work long hours without getting fatigued and go a long time without feeling hunger. Iboga also opens the body to the euphoria of spiritual dimension and is classified as a hallucinogen. The psychoactive substance found in the plant's root is called Ibogaine. In the early '60s, anecdotal reports appeared about its effectiveness in treating traumas and addictions of all kinds. Research into its anti-addictive properties came to a virtual halt in this country after the passage of the Controlled Substances Act in 1970. But Ibogaine is currently being used in clinics in 12 countries on six continents to facilitate detoxification and chemical dependence from substances such as methadone, heroine, alcohol, cocaine, and methamphetamine. The programs all include psychological introspection and spiritual awareness.

> "Everything and everyone that exists in the universe is filled with his or her own spirit, which can help us heal ourselves, heal each other, and heal the planet."

Grandmother Bernadette explains that, "Iboga is a cultural treasure, and it is a crucial ingredient in allowing us to get rid of the blocks within ourselves, get past emotional memories, and help resolve all conflicts." Well known in her country, she has been president of the health department of traditional medicine since 1994. Grandmother Bernadette says, "When the Grandmothers speak, the president listens. There is war all around us, but there is no war in Gabon."

Everything and everyone that exists in the universe is filled with his or her own spirit, which can help us heal ourselves, heal each other, and heal the planet.

Shamanic healers exist in every culture, and they all have an appreciation for the spirit in all things. They connect to that energy and use it to help people through the hard times. You can feel that spirit if you look at the world with an energetic perspective.

Chapter 4

Healing in Community

W**e are all tribal people.** It is an essential part of our humanity to be connected to someone other than ourselves. It is how we come into the world, and it is in our nature to gather in community, to celebrate joys as well as commiserate in sorrow. Our ancestors knew that when people came together in community, it lifted their spirits. The warmth of human contact reminds us that we are not alone in the world.

If you get sick, you heal better in community. When families, neighbors, and clans come together and push toward a common goal, it actually makes that outcome more likely to happen. Why? Because everyone has a stake in the outcome. The dreams and prayers of individual are magnified when people dream together. Gathering together in community is the core experience of all tribal cultures. It provides the structure, rituals, and ceremonies that bind people together.

In modern medicine, we're not healing in community. Instead, we heal privately in private rooms with privacy rules. What is a healing community? One where the people you hang out with share common values, respect each other, and contribute to it. A healing community is one in which everyone contributes their strengths, qualities, and beliefs, all expressed in the group's life as a whole. Healthy communities can be with people who live close and often see each other, or with those who can only get together periodically. Healthy communities can be with people, places, ancestors, or even unseen spirits, and always occur in a place where your inner strivings and external surroundings give you a sense of peace and belonging.

> "The warmth of human contact reminds us that we are not alone in the world."

One such community is that of the Oregon Country Fair (OCF) family. The OCF is a once-a-year gathering just outside Eugene, Oregon. Founded in 1969 by political activists, flower children, and environmentalists, this counterculture festival still meets every year on the weekend following the Fourth of July. At this time, it works to fulfill its credo to "create events and experiences that nurture the spirit, explore living artfully and authentically on earth, and transform culture in magical, joyous, and healthy ways."

Tens of thousands of visitors come every day throughout the long weekend to listen to the music and watch the parades, kid's theater, mimes, and stilt walkers. In addition, they listen to world recognized authorities on healthcare, politics, alternative fuels, and sustainability. The OCF has an elected board that administers its affairs, but it is the "family" of 6000 volunteers who run the actual event.

A pre-fair crew comes together weeks before setting up the 280 acre fairground and feeding the volunteers. A post-fair crew will stay a week afterward to close it down. Volunteers staff the presses and provide for healthcare, entertainment, security, traffic, and recycling. To become part of the OCF family means to be invited by someone already working on a crew. Every crew does its own hiring. To come aboard, someone typically knows you, how good of a worker you are, and how much you love the OCF.

I started coming to the OCF when I was already an elder. All of my daughters went, one since the '80s, and it has gradually evolved into a three-generation family reunion. We now go as an entire family to join a family camp. We are an extended family of about 50 people from infants to septuagenarians who are musicians, healers of every description, pilots, organic farmers, students, lawyers, teachers, carpenters, authors, and world travelers. We sleep in tents, tipis, and campers around one central fireplace.

DR. H AS THE TRUTH FAIRY

During the day, our jobs range from security, traffic, entertainment, administration, and recycling. Everyone works. The fair closes to the public every evening at 7:00 P.M. when it is "swept" by security. A line of hundreds moves through every public area clearing out anyone without fair-family identification, which is harder to get than courtside seats to an L.A. Laker's playoff game.

After 7:00 P.M., it's family time, and a carnival of color begins with costumes, music, dancing, and improvisational theater. Sometimes I reprise the role of the "Truth Fairy," a ballerina in pink tights and a tutu, a curly wig, and a red, clown nose. The Truth Fairy is the provider of truthful answers to life's critical questions. I am always accompanied by My Fair Brother, a retired airline pilot dressed as a giant blueberry. Sometimes another equally outrageous clown joins us as well. They enthusiastically announce my arrival. They lead the Truth Fairy into the fairgrounds with signs and fanfare, yelling "make way for Truth Fairy! The Truth Fairy has arrived and has the answer to an important question, problem, or predicament you may be facing. Is there something you want to know but may have been afraid to ask? Come on family, you know you want an answer. Three minutes with the Truth Fairy could change your life!" And so the rap goes on.

We set up some poles and connect them with "Do Not Cross" tape, leaving a narrow entry way and creating an 8-square-foot enclosure with a narrow

entry containing two chairs. People line up, because a 6-foot-6-inch fairy ballerina is no threat. You can pay attention or ignore the ridiculousness of the
scene, but for me, it's a chance to let my spontaneity emerge. I open a channel
into my unconscious mind and trust that my intuitive soul will flow and connect with someone else's in such a way that promotes healing.

Amazing things happen! A middle-aged, bright,
well-spoken, and heavily-accented Chinese woman once sat down. She said that before she asked
me anything, she wanted to know who I was and
why I was doing this. I wanted to honor this Orien-
tal greeting style and told her that I was a doctor of
the mind, but my real gift was in healing the soul.
"I am like a Ji Tong," I told her as she stared at me
blankly. "Ji Tong," I repeated, "the rural Chinese
folk healers who treat people by channeling the

spirits of dead Buddhist priests." She laughed, "Oh, you mean jitong," which
she pronounced completely differently. "You are a magician!"

A couple of minutes had passed, and there was a line of people waiting, so I
said, "Maybe this formal introduction has something to do with the question you wanted to ask me?" "Maybe," she said. She told me she was dating
an Occidental man who was ready for a more committed relationship, but she
wanted to go slower and get to know him better. The Truth Fairy said, "Look
at what just happened here. We knew nothing about each other a couple of
minutes ago, and yet we have already made a soulful connection. Maybe, just
like this moment, now is the right time and the right place to make a more
spontaneous connection."

She paused and finally said, "But I am afraid that if I make this jump, I may
fall." The Truth Fairy said, "You will land or you will learn to fly. Trust your
heart. It knows things your mind can't fathom, and it will give you an opportunity to write a new ending to your old story." Then, time was up. We hugged
and said, "Goodbye."

A young man, perhaps in his mid-twenties, followed her and got down on
his knees to bow before entering the space. He sat down and asked, "Truth
Fairy, what is the secret of my life?" I responded that if he had to ask me, the
likelihood was small that he couldn't hear the answer. While he was formu-
lating a response, I asked him, "What was the bowing entrance all about?" He
said he thought that was how one was supposed to enter into the presence of
the truth. I said that what he thought had nothing to do with my expectation or me, but I had the feeling his bowing entry may be related to a bigger
question in his life right now. "What's that?" He asked. I said, "When facing
uncertainty, your way of getting comfortable is to take control. What's the

uncomfortable situation you're in now?" He said he was in a relationship with a woman that he thought he wanted to stay with, but such a decision would dramatically change his lifestyle. "Maybe it's time to trust the process rather than control the outcome," the Truth Fairy said.

I got up to hug him goodbye, but he didn't want to leave. He had another question for me as I was ushering him out. "How do I let go?" He wanted to know. I said, "That's the secret." He wanted me to tell him, but that he had to discover himself.

Next, a woman in her late fifties told me she was a nurse with Stage IV breast cancer. She was working regularly but becoming increasingly preoccupied with the fear that her cancer was catching up with her. I said the more time she spent looking over her shoulder, the bigger that fear monster would get. "It's like looking at your life through the rearview mirror; it always makes objects appear larger than they are." Instead, I told her to look straight ahead. "Look at what you're doing. Look at the impact you have on others by sharing your gifts. Your cancer doesn't define who you are any more than the people you touch. Tell your story every day because that's what we want to leave behind."

This is how we heal in community. The right people, in the right place, at the right time. You get to see the world from a different perspective.

Every year, I take away from this healing community an appreciation of tolerance, of the many ways there are to serve humanity and to show love to one another. With thousands of people camping in close quarters and standing in line to go potty, OCF is a place where judgment is suspended and peace reigns. Here, for at least a little while, I feel the truth of Native American wisdom that if you can remember the stories your great-grandfathers told and tell them to your grandchildren, your tribe lives for another seven generations.

Healing communities can also be created around tragedy and common suffering. People come together to face cancer, addictions, and traumas because we heal better in community. For example, a friend sent me this story from the Detroit News in April of 2007, which tells the story of Miles Levin, an 18-year-old young man who was living with a rare pediatric cancer called Rhabdomyosarcoma. Miles was 16 when he was diagnosed with this highly malignant cancer of the soft tissues, which had advanced over the last two years. Miles decided to document his life's journey on the pages of an online healing community, www.carepages.com.

Here are some of Miles's entries:

For awhile now, with every significant event or experience that's come along on the journey I call my life, I have had to consider, "Am I going to share this?" This is not my diary, but I believe candor is courage. In light of this, I've decided to share something with you, which I normally keep to myself. I was asked what college I was going to by a friend tonight. Now I can say I know what it feels like to be harpooned in the chest. He is one of the most well-meaning people I know, so I wasn't quite sure what his words meant. Anyway, I had to tell them I'm not going to college in the fall. Though I didn't want to say it outright because it would almost feel explicit, it doesn't look like I'm going to college in the spring either or in any subsequent fall.

It is not dying that scares me, it's dying and having no impact. I know a lot of eyes are watching me suffer, and win or lose, this is my time for impact.

I feel relatively ready. I'm proud of myself, proud of my life, and proud of the story of my life. I say the story because it includes everybody in it and all the goodness and courage displayed by my family, the generosity of people... I'm proud of the people my friends have become. They've grown so tall. I am proud of myself. What I've done I believe is what I've been sent here to do. Something has shifted. Everything is okay now. It's okay because I am OK with it. Thank goodness that my having and dying from cancer impacts the lives of so many thousands of people that it overshadows any personal bad. I'm in escalating pain, but I hardly mind. You know why? Because this is my story, and it's not meant to be told any other way.

"Thank goodness that my having and dying from cancer impacts the lives of so many thousands that it overshadows any personal bad. I'm in escalating pain, but I hardly mind...this is my story, and it's not meant to be told any other way."

-Miles

I was moved by his candor and wisdom, which seemed beyond his years, and wrote to him regularly on his care page.

A month before his death, he went away to a camp exclusively for boys with cancer. He said that totally contrary to what you might expect at the camp, it had nonstop energy with vitality bursting from its victims. Miles said the best part of being there was, "Everybody here gets it, and that's not something you can experience with your regular friends."

On his return from the camp, he wrote that without a working treatment plan, his remaining time may be short. "My time left is probably two to five weeks," he said. "I'm trying to relax. I know I've fought my very best, and now it's up to greater powers, whether they be divine or forces of nature. I find myself altering between feelings of gratitude for all that my life has been and wishing to trade it all for a normal, obscure teenage existence."

At the end, Miles wrote on his care page, which by now had become a bill-board for a worldwide audience, "I know I'll never be happy with this update because there's no way to say thank you, it's so huge, but not to try to say it would be worse. It's a stupid system, but the only way to fully understand what you have is by losing it. Therefore, luckily for me, that's something I will never know.... I am blessed to be enveloped in love that I will never lose."

I wrote a final farewell to Miles in which I reminded him that he told us his greatest fear was not dying, but dying "without having had an impact." I told him not to worry because his life was an inspiration to people all over the world. I told him, "You bear witness to how to live every day in the moment and make every day worth remembering. I remember you, Miles, in all those moments I find myself enveloped in love that I will never lose."

Like pain and suffering, acts of terror can also build healing communities. I spoke at the Anaheim Convention Center to 4,000 university-based IT specialists on the one-year anniversary of the worst campus killings in American history, the Virginia Tech massacre of April 2007. People from Virginia Tech were in the audience. Thirty-two victims were killed and two dozen others wounded by a mentally disturbed student, who then killed himself. The massacre was the deadliest peacetime shooting incident by a single gunman in United States history.

One of the students killed was a young woman, 18-year-old Austin Cloyd, the daughter of Brian Cloyd, an accounting professor at Virginia Tech. After the tragedy, contributions were sent in her name. Professor Clyde and his wife asked that they be sent in Austin's name to the Appalachia Service Project (ASP), a nonprofit organization that repairs dilapidated houses in the poorest parts of Appalachia. Austin had a passion for social justice. She made four week-long trips with ASP, and those trips shaped her life, instilling the desire to pursue a career in social services.

Since ASP's founding in 1969, the organization has helped repair more than 13,000 homes in Virginia, Kentucky, Tennessee, and West Virginia. For all those years, volunteers came mostly from church groups. The Cloyds got the college community to support the project. To the Cloyds' surprise, the program almost immediately received nearly $70,000 in gifts. Dr. Cloyd began organizing trips for students and faculty to participate on five weekend house repair trips. In his classroom, Dr. Cloyd shifted from his typical focus on taxes and offered an honors class titled, "Inventing the Future Through our 'Ur Prosim' Tradition," a reference to Virginia Tech University's motto, "That I May Serve." Students in the class spend one week working with the ASP.

At the same time I was speaking in Anaheim about the importance of authentic human connections in the Facebook age, the Internet weapons dealer who had shipped one of the guns used in the massacre spoke on the Virginia Tech campus. The Students for Concealed Carry on Campus (SCCC) invited Eric Thompson, owner of the online gun dealership, TGSCOM, to the campus. Mr. Thompson told the audience that what he did was within the letter of the law. He sold it to the dealer who then sold it to the killer but only after he had submitted his information for a background check and passed. Mr. Thompson said that not only did he do nothing wrong, but to some extent, he too was a victim. He also said that the bad publicity has hurt his businesses. One of Thompson's companies also sold two handgun magazines and a holster to Stephen Kazmierczak, who killed five Northern Illinois University students and then himself just two months before.

His presence on the campus offended me, at the very least. It was incredibly insensitive to the families of the victims still recovering from the horrendous tragedy. But Thompson was invited by VT students who believed that carrying weapons on campus actually reduced the odds that some madman might victimize them. The SCCC believed no one should be left without recourse other than hiding under his or her desk waiting and praying not to be killed. They wanted to arm themselves.

Roughly, here were the choices. One could use this tragedy as motivation to carry concealed weapons, arming oneself against a conspiratorial world of potential assassins, or one could honor Austin Cloyd's memory and break away from the world of dread. Here's a community that voted to heal by disarming themselves and reaching out to others.

Imagine...

A local hospital that brings a community together by mobilizing all of its healing practitioners, ranging from Native American healers, energy and body workers, nutritional experts, dance/play/art therapists, and multimedia artists whose talents often go unappreciated and untapped.

Imagine...

A small city hospital that sees itself not only as an acute care facility but a community resource that addresses the community's broader health needs.

A visionary hospital CEO in a small Midwestern town invited me to join him in sharing his vision of community health. He wanted to move his board and hospital staff into a more proactive, collaborative, and integrated model of

"Imagine…

A small city

hospital that

sees itself not

only as an

acute care

facility but a

community

resource that

addresses the

community's

broader health

needs."

healthcare delivery. I spent a year consulting in Red Wing, Minnesota, a picture-postcard Mississippi River town of 17,000. In the mid-nineteenth century, Scandinavian and German immigrants arrived on riverboats. Chief Red Wing of the local Mdewankanton Lakota tribe, who had been living there for eons, welcomed them in peace and friendship.

The overwhelming majority of Red Wing's population is still the multigenerational descendants of those original settlers. The town is largely white and Protestant and still sits right next to Red Wing's descendants on the Prairie Island Indian Community. Chief Red Wing may have welcomed the settlers in friendship, but there was probably tension between the communities from the beginning. The profitable casino, Treasure Island Casino and Resort, the town's largest employer, intensifies those tensions today. The tribe's wealth has funded many tribal improvements and provided every tribal member with a significant yearly income. Children under 18 have the money kept in a trust fund available to them in a lump sum when they come of legal age. The tribe has also provided Red Wing with a new ice hockey arena among other public works.

Like other small tribes who were fortunate enough to find themselves near cities, Red Wing's newfound wealth came with some untoward consequences. For example, Native American kids were dropping out of school at an alarming rate and alcohol use, drug abuse, and gang involvement was increasing. With guaranteed per capita income and young Indians driving fancy cars and pickups, adolescent tensions intensified.

During that year, I met with the hospital staff, the board, political and business leaders, educators, police, social service agencies, and the Prairie Island Indian Community to get a sense of their support of this vision of community health. I also spoke to the entire population in the town's historic theater about the future of healthcare and the critical importance of moving from the current paradigm of an interventional model to a preventative one.

Dr. H. and the Mayor of Red Wing

The CEO invited medical staff, administrators, and program managers to a daylong retreat entitled, "An Experiential Gift." For a day, they experienced hands-on demonstrations by art, music, massage and movement therapists, and energy and meditation practitioners. They experienced Feldenkreis, yoga, painting, acupressure, and therapeutic massage. Those contacts resulted in some of these practitioners being included into existing hospital programs.

The growing Hispanic community said getting a Spanish-speaking priest in the city would make the greatest impact in healthcare delivery. The priest would have the most direct access to people in need. They would hear ev-

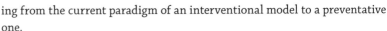

erything and could introduce social services and health care options before people appeared in emergency rooms and police stations. Red Wing citizens petitioned the Catholic Archbishop in Minneapolis/St. Paul to find a priest for them. The hospital invited Winfred Red Cloud, a spiritual leader, to perform a blessing ceremony at the hospital's rededication event. Winfred Red Cloud is the great grandson of Chief Red Cloud, chief of the Oglala Lakota and the only Native American leader to win a major war against the United States.

Winfred Red Cloud performed the blessing ceremony, which was photographed and reported in the local paper. One result was an invitation to perform a blessing ceremony at a local middle school, which was also having a retention problem with Indian students. I thought this was a great idea and imagined young Indians watching their traditions respected and elders honored would be a positive experience. An announcement was sent home with the children telling parents that Mr. Winfred Red Cloud, the distinguished Lakota spiritual leader, would be performing a blessing ceremony at the school. It welcomed parents to attend on Tuesday at 2:45 P.M.

The night before the blessing ceremony, the school board was holding its regularly scheduled meeting. The board was greeted by a small but vocal group of protesters who objected to the following day's scheduled ceremony. They argued that it was a violation of church and state separation and that the next thing might be priests conducting communion services. They threatened legal action if the ceremony was held. Lawyers were consulted that night, and the decision was made to cancel the ceremony.

To reject a blessing is a sign of disrespect and ridicule, and the Prairie Island Lakota were plenty pissed off. But instead of intensifying cultural antagonisms, something extraordinary happened. Prominent representatives of Red Wing's citizenry signed a letter that appeared in the local paper, apologizing for the school board's decision. They were asking for the tribe's blessings just as their ancestors had been blessed when they first arrived.

The hospital CEO was among those who delivered the letter to the Tribal Council. When the healthcare contract came up a year later with a hospital in a city 60 miles away, the community decided not to renew it. Its community members, by and large, now go to Red Wing Hospital because its sensitivity and openness had impressed them.

Red Wing became a true community hospital.

DR. H. IN RED WING WITH ONE OF THE CITY'S FIREMEN

It reached out into the community to get its members healthy and involved instead of waiting for them to show up in the emergency rooms as is often seen in our current model of healthcare.

Like Red Wing, the Roxbury section of Boston, Massachusetts is another paradigm-shifting community health model. Every week, a clinic is conducted in a converted RV called The Family Van. It parks in the same place on the same day of the week, and people come to see healthcare providers, all of whom are certified professionals but not medical doctors. Some providers receive additional training to provide medicines, but they all have long conversations and develop personal relationships with their patients.

The Family Van is a non-profit organization affiliated with Harvard Medical School and provides low-cost, portable screening tools for diabetes, obesity, hypertension, alcohol abuse, and depression. They treat patients with these chronic diseases for preventative check-ups. In 2009, The Family Van saved the healthcare system of Boston more than $20 million, and it did it on a meager budget of $500,000. The Family Van has expanded access, controlled costs, and created a healing community. There are now more than 2,000 mobile health clinics across the United States.

A more structurally permanent inner city, community-based health clinic is

being built in Philadelphia. This architecturally innovative building is called the Patch Adams Free Clinic. For a small annual fee, members will get everything from urgent care, chronic care, counseling, birthing, family planning, chiropractic services, acupuncture, yoga, massage, and after-school clubs.

The Patch Adams Free Clinic, the brainchild of Paul Glover, a community organizer and social entrepreneur, was first launched as an alternative health insurance program in upstate New York called the Ithaca Health Fund. The fund, now in its twelfth year, is available to individuals for $100 a year and is built on the old-fashioned barter system. The doctors, dentists, massage therapists, physical therapists, yoga instructors, farmers, midwives, lawyers, and musicians all contribute their services to get paid in "money" that Glover prints.

PATCH ADAMS AND DR. H.

The monetary system is guaranteed by human activity. Every note entitles the bearer to receive a specified number of hours in labor or a negotiated value in goods or services. The Ithaca Health Fund has seen thousands of people trading millions of dollars of this "money," all of which is recycled within the

Healing In Community

community. This is clearly more than a health facility. The clinic is an economic development model curing existing medical problems and building community soul.

I want to support Paul Glover's vision of the Patch Adams Free Clinic bringing the first Patch Adams Full Moon Festival (PAFMF) to Philadelphia. The PAFMF was born in the wee hours of many hilarious mornings on the road with Patch. We envisioned a health promotion event and massive fundraiser to support a city's preventative health services, such as free clinics, homeless shelters, AIDS hospices, after-school programs, senior centers, Meals-on-Wheels, and similar programs.

A long, full moon weekend would bring a whole city together to share resources. People from diverse backgrounds would share their experience, wisdom, and healing stories including doctors, dentists, midwives, and survivors of cancer, addictions, traumas, burns, autoimmune diseases, depression, ADD, and PTSD. Together they would tell each other what has worked and what hasn't.

"Nobody makes it's alone. Find a community, a place that inspires and lifts your spirit. Such a community will remind you of what you like best about who you are..."

Imagine a gathering where there is an opportunity to listen to the stories of parents with ADD kids who found alternatives to medicating them. Picture Native American veterans, welcomed home in traditional warrior ceremonies resulting in rarely seen cases of PTSD, offering healing sweat lodge ceremonies to returning Iraq and Afghan veterans, among whom PTSD is an epidemic. Visualize adult children and primary caretakers of aging parents helping each other expand their resources.

For these weekends, Patch would bring in clowns from all over the world to visit hospitals, hospices, and shelters and to paint murals on dilapidated walls. They would be joined by performances from world-class musicians and entertainers. Patch would close the event by inviting people to participate in the world's largest mooning. The PAFMF is a chance to remind each other of our noblest selves, to come together for the joyful expectation that something good is going to happen. It is a chance for a community creating passionate energy to celebrate life and lift the human spirit, renewing the bonds that bind people together.

Nobody makes it's alone. Find a community, a place that inspires and lifts your spirit. Such a community will remind you of what you like best about who you are and allow you to share yourself more fully.

Chapter 5

Radical Self-Acceptance

L iving the good life has nothing to do with whether you are born with a silver spoon or if you've had to survive enormous hardship. Whatever hand life deals you turns out to be less important than the choices you make about playing the hand you've been dealt. A quality life has nothing to do with being dealt perfect cards, but has to do with learning how to play an imperfect hand well. Destiny is the hand that you're dealt; free will is how you choose to play it. Choice is our greatest power because it gives you an opportunity to move beyond the powerlessness of your predicament. If you believe you have no choice and are so gripped by fear that it immobilizes you, then your only hope is to wait for something or someone other than yourself to bail you out. St. George may miraculously appear and slay your dragon – miracles do happen – but you've surrendered your destiny to someone else's control.

If you can find a way to be fully present with who are and where you find yourself, then you can choose to take one step to live a quality life. If you can't, you will stay immobilized by your resentment, rage, and despair. Only when you own the hand you've been dealt, can you play it well. This is radical self-acceptance.

ROGER EBERT

I remember Roger Ebert as the short, chubby partner in that great film critic duo, Siskel and Ebert. Roger Ebert was sharp, witty, and literate, with big-rimmed eyeglasses that made him look owlishly professional. I hadn't seen him in years, but in March 2010, I saw him on "The Oprah Winfrey Show." It wasn't the Roger from my memory; his face was thinner, scarred, and he spoke with a synthesized voice.

In 2002, Roger had surgery for thyroid cancer and thought they had gotten it all. The following year, they found the cancer in his salivary gland, which they took out and then irradiated. All during this time, Roger continued to work, writing his column in *The Chicago Sun-Times* and through his blogs.

In 2006, doctors removed his right jaw after which followed a series of reconstructive procedures and complications. Since 2006, Roger has not eaten or drank anything by mouth. He is fed through a gravity-drip bag through a permanent opening into his stomach. He says he does not miss the activity of eating or drinking so much as he misses the camaraderie of dining with friends.

Roger revealed all this in the February 2010 issue of Esquire Magazine in an in-depth interview, which incorporated a full-page portrait of his surgically-altered face. Roger's doctors have asked him to let them make another attempt at restoring his jaw and voice, but Roger has refused. He says, "I'm done with surgery, even if the cancer returns. This is who I am, this is how I look, and I'm okay with dying. I was perfectly content before I was born, and I'm thinking of death as the same state. I hope to be spared as much pain as possible on the approach path."

Roger said it was time that people looked at his face. "This is the way I look. I don't have a perfect face, but my life is happy and productive. We have to find peace with the way we look and get on with life."

Roger's appearance on Oprah's show was the first time he had spoken publicly in four years. He spoke in his synthesized voice that he calls "Roger Junior." Computer programmers compiled his DVD commentaries to capture the essence of his voice and recreated it. Roger says, "It needs a little improvement, but it sounds like me, and talking makes me happy. In the first grade, they said I talked too much, and I still can." This is radical self-acceptance.

Here's another example. On the front page of the style section of The New York Times in May of 2007 was a photograph of a young woman dancing in a Los Angeles nightclub in a mini-skirt and a prosthetic leg. The thigh looked like an elongated crystal ball, and the lower leg had a spike attached to a sandal-strapped foot.

The woman was Sarah Reinertsen, a 32-year-old athlete whose left leg was amputated above the knee when she was seven years old, the result of a tissue defect with which she was born. She is a track star who was a contestant on CBS's "Amazing Race" and the first woman to compete in the Ironman Kona on a prosthesis. She has also competed in marathons in New York, L.A., New Zealand, and London.

In the article, Sarah explained her love to compete against the "able-bodied." "I get a thrill when I pass two-legged people," said Sarah. "People will always stare; it's human nature, and it's tough to be this animal in a zoo." She turned the tables though, and said, "This is who I am. If you have a problem with that, it's your problem, not mine. As soon as people stop looking at the disability as a total tragedy, they can ask about the cool leg I'm wearing." This is radical self-acceptance.

I was taught not to look at disabled people. "Don't stare," my mother would whisper and nudge. However, I never realized that my ignoring them encouraged the disabled to cover it up themselves. I learned this from my friend Michael Aronin, a great standup comic who has cerebral palsy and is severely spastic. Michael knows people look at him as he jerks around and talks a bit funny, so he disarms them. I heard him tell a group as he flailed out onto the stage, "I don't like flying anymore; I get stopped in airports, and they ask me if I'm a Northwest pilot. And kids will ask you anything. I tell them this is what happens to you if you watch too much Barney." Michael says, "When people see me for the first time, they see I'm OK with being me."

Sarah and Michael are teaching us all not to run and hide from ourselves, but rather, to say, "Look at me. I am my own best friend." Or as the Zulu proverb teaches, if there is no enemy within, the enemy outside can do you no harm.

Martha Mason's story is another example. I was introduced to her story through an obituary in The New York Times in May of 2009. Martha died in her home in Lattimore, North Carolina, at the age of 71. This remarkable woman was struck by polio when she was 11. She went to bed one night feeling achy, but didn't tell her parents about it because they had just buried her 13-year-old brother who had died of polio only days before.

Lattimore has been home to Martha her entire life, and for 60 of those years, she lived in an iron lung, longer than anyone has before. Maybe this small town, where people have known you and your family for generations, is the only place she could have thrived so well. Being encased in a 7-foot-long, 800-pound iron cylinder made it hard to move around easily, so in a town of 400 people, Martha didn't have to go to town. Instead, the town came to her. In Lattimore, everyone was a neighbor. Her teachers came to her, the family doctor made housecalls, and members of the fire department came by during terrible weather and power failures to make sure her backup generator was working.

Martha Mason came home to Lattimore after her diagnoses, graduated number one in her high school and university class, and then began writing for the local newspaper. High school graduates would stop by before graduation so Martha could admire them in their caps and gowns. Newly-married couples came by in their wedding finery, and town celebrations always included her. She became an associate professor of communications at Wake Forest University and had friends all over the world who sent her magnets to stick on her iron lung. Martha often gave dinner parties where she ate lying down with her guests around the dinner table. Pushed up beside the table, her iron lung looked "like a steamer trunk."

Fifty years later, using a voice activated computer, Martha wrote a book about her life (*Breath*, Down-Home Press, 2003). Martha said she survived because she was endlessly curious, and there was so much to learn. She chose to remain in an iron lung because of the freedom it gave her. Martha didn't want to try one of the newer, smaller ventilators because it might require tubes in her throat. She could live at home in a community that helped her to be independent because the iron lung didn't require professional training to operate,

Anticipating every new day rather than dreading the coming dawn is radical self-acceptance. Martha Mason said, "I'm happy with who I am, and where I am. I wouldn't have chosen this life, certainly. But given this life, I probably had the best situation anyone could ask for... a fine and full life." This is radical self-acceptance.

Here's a story about one of my heroes, Wilma Rudolph, the first American woman to win three Olympic gold medals. Wilma was number 20 of 22 children raised in rural Tennessee by poor, hard-working people. She contracted polio at a young age, which left her left leg and foot weak and deformed. Discouraged by local doctors who told Wilma she would never walk again, her mother took her twice a week by bus to Nashville, some 50 miles away. After several years of intense physical therapy, massage, and the support of a metal leg brace, Wilma got well.

Wilma started playing basketball in high school. She was so fast that they called her "Skeeter," which was short for mosquito. A Tennessee State University track coach watched her play and encouraged her high school basketball coach to form a girl's track team. She was undefeated at her high school track events and received a full scholarship to Tennessee State where she was a collegiate world-record holder. She then moved on to Olympic fame in Rome in 1960 and became a worldwide celebrity.

After graduation, Wilma became a schoolteacher, track coach, and civil rights activist, but she said her greatest accomplishment was the establishment of the Wilma Rudolph Foundation, a community-based non-profit outreach program to nurture young students and athletes

When Wilma was in her early fifties, she was diagnosed with a malignant brain tumor and died within a year. During the last year of her life, exhausted by her treatment, she still managed to visit schools in rural Tennessee. Wilma spoke to poor, underachieving kids and told them that the most important lesson she learned in life, she learned in track. And that lesson was, "Don't ever drop out of a race, because if you drop out once, it's easier to drop out twice." Wilma told these children that they were in the race of their lives, and to stay in school because then they would be prepared to be strong finishers in life.

This is the difference between healing and curing. Wilma Rudolph was not cured of her disease, but she was healed. Healing is a spiritual expedition not a physical one. It's about connecting personally with something other than yourself. Healing is about getting hooked up to some energetic power source that reminds you that whatever you're facing, you're not facing it alone. Healing is having the courage to see yourself as you are and still loving yourself. The process of healing is not about getting cured, it's about getting real. And getting real is radical self-acceptance.

Even in dementia one can find acceptance. I read about Doris and Ethel in my local paper. Both in their eighties, they shared a room in an assisted living facility for people with moderate to severe dementia. Neither of them knew why they lived there or how they got there. They didn't remember names or faces. Reality was sometimes elusive, but they knew each other.

Doris and Ethel were nurses; both lived through the Great Depression, World War II, had lost husbands, and had children and grandchildren. They were best friends and passed their days making hats and talking to each other. They never ran out of things to say, and they loved to knit hats. It took them a couple of days to knit each colorful hat, but on completion, each was donated to the Salvation Army, which distributed them at a homeless shelter.

These handmade hats were deeply appreciated, and sometimes Doris and Ethel received thank you notes and photos from grateful recipients. Both of them said this was their family, and looking at those cards and pictures made them cry. These two old ladies are taking care of each other; they aren't cured, but they are healed.

Terminal illness is another opportunity for radical self-acceptance. I met Mattie Stepanek the year before he died of a rare form of muscular dystrophy called Dysautonomic Mitochondrial Myopathy. He had a sister and two brothers who also died from the disease. To cope with the death of his older brother when he was three, Mattie started writing poetry. By the time he was 12, he had written five books of poetry that had made The New York Times Bestseller List. He appeared on "The Oprah Winfrey Show," "Larry King Live," "Good Morning America," and became National Goodwill Ambassador for the Muscular Dystrophy Association. His story was chronicled in newspapers and magazines all over the world.

Mattie wanted most to be remembered as an international peace advocate. I met him at a National Caring Award ceremony at the Kennedy Center in 2003, where he was introducing his hero, former President Jimmy Carter. Mattie rolled out on stage in a wheelchair accompanied by his service dog,

Radical Self Acceptance

Micah, breathing through a tracheotomy tube attached to a ventilator. He was self-effacing, had a sense of humor, and seemed confident and happy. When Jimmy Carter took the stage, he thanked Mattie and said he had traveled to 122 foreign countries, met kings and queens, but that Mattie Stepanek was the most extraordinary person he had ever met.

I was introduced to Mattie afterward, and like everyone else, was taken by his precociousness and old-soul quality. Later, I asked his mother what she thought it was about him that inspired such profound connections with people. She said, "Mattie just gives people something to believe in; I think that's why he's here."

Mattie died a couple of weeks before his 14th birthday. Nearly 1,350 people, among them Oprah Winfrey and Jimmy Carter, who delivered the eulogy, attended his funeral. Firefighters, whom he loved, stood as an honor-guard outside the church. His casket was covered with Harley-Davidson and firefighter bumper stickers and was draped in the flag of the United Nations. Mattie's mother wrote, "You are my best friend, and I always have been and always will be proud of you, my son. Thank you for the coffee, the foot massages, the snuggles, the conversations, the inspiration, the motivation, the laughter, the tears, the prayers, the dreams you shared, and for the gift of celebrating life."

"Balance between inner vision and outer reality is how we live in peace with ourselves and leave an imprint on others."

Balance between inner vision and outer reality is how we live in peace with ourselves and leave an imprint on others. Five years after his death, people keep coming to Mattie's website, Mattieonline.com. They keep his message of hope and peace in the world alive for him. Visitors come to Mattie Stepanek Park in Rockville, MD, where a bronze statue of him with Micah at his side sits in the middle of Peace Garden. On 26 acres, the park has ball fields, picnic areas, and jogging trails. Sprinkled around the spacious green space are benches and plaques with quotes from Mattie's books and speeches and paved paths of bricks inscribed with messages from supporters.

But you don't have to be confronting imminent mortality before you can identify your strengths and come to peace with your frailties. The only requirements for this kind of self-awareness is a willingness to look directly at who you are and let go of what else you thought you needed to be so that you can get on with the rest of your life.

Getting old is the mechanism by which we are forced to tame our egos. If we cannot let go of the image we once had of ourselves and own the truth of who we are now, then it reduces the length and quality of our lives.

I'm old and getting older. My grandkids tell me I was born "B.D," – before dinosaurs – but I'm still active, and my spirit is strong. The process of aging has been a struggle though. I still have trouble letting go of the internalized image I have of what it means to be a strong and competent man. My body is slowing down, I stay sore longer, and I can't pee my name in the snow; I'm happy if I can clear my toes. I focus on my losses because they raise the ugly head of my worst fears – losing my mind, becoming immobilized or burdensome.

To be in a place of radical self-acceptance is to let go of any old images that no longer serve one. This is an ongoing struggle for me, because every time I get to a place where I can love the one I'm with, something happens to remind me I still have a long way to go.

A couple of years ago, my wife and I decided to downsize, which would allow us to support our lifestyle, but I was unprepared for the consequences of that decision. I have always been able to deal with losses of loved ones and body functions, but I lost my equilibrium as I prepared to my leave my home of 40 years. This was not just a house; this was the ceremonial center of a multi-generational family, an extension of my body and soul. Four generations had slept within its walls, and our life history was inside and on the surrounding grounds. My grandchildren's placentas were buried outside. Each had its own bush or tree on top of it. I was the keeper of a sweat lodge at my home.

I knew in my mind that the house did not hold the essence of me or what we experienced there as family, but as I went through my library and had to decide which books to keep or give away, I wept. When they put the for sale sign out in front, which summarized that part of my life history as "4BR, 3B, 5 fireplaces, separate guest house," I got depressed.

My friend and holy brother, Patch Adams, came to visit me, and we talked long into the night surrounded by my treasures. Patch looked at me in my misery and said that whatever else moving from this house meant for me, moving also released me from the inertia of its comforts, which may have kept me from exploring some new territory. And then he recited this poem, one of his favorite pastimes, by Mary Oliver:

> To live in this world you must be able to do three things:
> to love what is mortal;
> to hold it
> against your bones knowing
> your own life depends on it;
> and, when the time comes to let it go,
> to let it go.

An excerpt of "In Blackwater Woods," from American Primitive by Mary Oliver, 1983.

Radical Self Acceptance

And slowly I came back among the living. We don't take anything with us. Everything that's really important, we leave behind. The most important question in life is how well did you love.

Chapter 6

Symbols, Rituals, and Ceremonies

Everything on the face of the planet has its own intrinsic value maintaining harmony on the planet. Every stone, plant, and creature has evolved with its own place and purpose. If such things hold a special significance for you, then in addition to its intrinsic value, it holds symbolic, even sacramental value. When you feel an intense connection, a kinship with something, whether it's a stone, scroll, tree, rattle, animal, or unseen ancestral spirit, then they possess an energy that can be harnessed to help you through hard times.

When those symbolic objects are used within the structure of a ritual or ceremony, we intensify the object's power. These symbols then become sacred because they connect us to something other than ourselves and remind us that whatever we face, we do not face it alone.

In the practice of modern medicine, we dramatically undervalue the ritual and ceremonial aspects of healing. Even though modern surgery has all the elements of a ceremony – the preparatory ablutions, special instruments, the induction of trance, and mastery of a special language – we do not typically see what goes on in that way. "That's not a ritual," we say because each of those actions, the hand washing, the surgical masks, the sophisticated machinery, all have a rational reason. It's not like rattles, feathers, wine, and wafers, which tap into something irrational so we say their impact is purely psychological, maybe even magical.

There is no difference between the psychological and physical body. Thoughts and feelings are real, measurable forces. Thoughts and feelings have power, and we can use them to design our reality rather than just react to it.

Quantum physicists and brain researchers support what mystics have been telling us for millennia. If enough minds share the same thought, we can create a universal, collective consciousness. Rituals, ceremonies, and the use of sacred symbolic objects can promote transformative change. They provide the structure that allows us to get in touch with the soul of our being. They tell a story that inspires us to see beyond our limitations.

My sacred objects range from scrolls and feathers to rattles and drums. I also have a special relationship with turtles and snakes, which represent wise messengers for me, maybe even guardian angels. Their appearances in my dreams or reality are a wakeup call and always get my attention. Turtles are a universally regarded symbol of fertility, growth, and wisdom. They are also a healing symbol; when a turtle is threatened, it seeks strength within. We need to do the same. When something threatens, we also need to go inside to get stronger. Going inside means getting your head, lips, and heart in balance. That's how we mobilize our strength. Then, like the turtle, if we want to move ahead and get beyond the threat, we have to take a risk and stick out our necks.

My snake messenger came to me during a pilgrimage to Bear Butte, South Dakota about 30 years ago. This is a sacred mountain for the Lakota and Cheyenne tribes of the Great Plains. This is where Chief Red Cloud came to seek vision and save his people, and where Native people from many tribes now come for vision quests.

I was in Rapid City for an Indian Health Service meeting, and Bear Butte was so close, I took the opportunity to bring my sacred instruments to this holy mountain to re-energize them. Bear Butte is now a public state park, but the sacred vision quest grounds at the mountaintop are still reserved for Native Americans. In the parking lot, I spread out the contents of my medicine box and picked out those items I intended to carry up. While carefully placing each item in my backpack, I saw a Native American family watching me from a distance. They approached me and asked if I was going to pray at the top. I told them I was, and they replied that they couldn't all get to the top. They asked me if I would say a prayer up there for their father who had just passed away. I said I would be honored, and they handed me a braid of sweet grass and told me something about their husband, father, and grandfather.

"…when a turtle is threatened, it seeks strength within. We need to do the same."

I was feeling good as I walked to my first stop, which was at the sweat lodge grounds at the base of the mountain. I loved the idea that this Jewish boy from N.Y.C. was asked to pray for my Native relatives. I tied my prayer bundles to the lodges and continued up the mountain. Still glowing in my self-satisfied reverie, I didn't see the rattlesnake right in front of me until I heard it rattle. Two feet in front of me, coiled and ready to strike, it made me catch my breath. I stepped back slowly, talking to the snake while retreating. "I know you were here first," I said. "This is your place. I'm just visiting and wasn't paying attention." I assured it that I was coming here from a good place, and finally, I was far enough back that the snake uncoiled and went away.

I reflected on that for a while when I reached the top of that monolith. I thought about how captivated I had become by my ego that I lost sight of where I fit into the scheme of things. This was never about me; I was picked

RATTLESNAKE SCULPTURE

out as a trustworthy messenger, and I was the instrument not the creator or architect, a transmitter through which their healing spirit flowed. This is usually how it is for me. It takes some kind of life-challenging confrontation to get my attention and change my behavior.

On that holy mountain, my snake relative reminded me to tame my ego. I have a sculpture of a rattlesnake that now hangs right in the middle of my diploma wall. When I look at it, it whispers in my ear, "Do not take yourself too seriously."

Just as I use symbols, rituals, and ceremonies for myself, I prescribe them for patients, students, and friends as well. I help them put together the elements that will help them become full participants in their own healing and in the healing of others.

Teryl "T." Johansson is a native Oregonian and a professional fly-fishing guide, among other things. I call her my River Sister. T. learned to fish at her father's knee when she was three years old. She once took a four-month solo fly-fishing trip on the West's best streams and wrote a book about it. I love her reverence of rivers, and we have been friends for over 20 years, connected by this love of the music of a moving line in the cathedral of nature.

A couple of years ago, T. wrote to me saying that she had just gotten a letter from her friend in Zürich, Switzerland, asking if she knew anything about a Dr. Hammerschlag, who with Native American healers, was conducting a workshop on ceremonial healing. He wanted to know if he should fly half-way around the world to attend. T. said, "He is a first-class schmuck. Save your

TERYL "T" JOHANSSON

money, bring me to Switzerland instead, and I'll teach you all you need to know about healing."

Only later did she add that if he came, she would come too, because we were brother and sister.

Just before the workshop, T. wrote to say that she wasn't coming because she'd just been diagnosed with anal cancer. For years, she'd been told it was only a persistent fissure, but now so far advanced, it required aggressive radiation and chemotherapy, almost surely followed by colostomy surgery. I told her to do what she needed to do at home because she would surely be with us in our circle anyway. She would feel our energy and prayers during her healing journey.

Symbols, Rituals and Ceremonies

As her grueling therapeutic course unfolded, she felt those vibes and got her community of friends to send her "butt blessings." In her weakest moments, this unseen but heartfelt community showed up. T. wrote, "You have empowered the warrior in me. I have become 98 pounds of hairless, fighting fury! After 24 doses of radiation, it's taking a toll on my tender tushy, which looks as if it's been dipped in a deep fat-fryer."

Post-treatment biopsies revealed residual cancer, and T. was now facing a life and death decision. She wrote, "Pray for me hard. It makes a difference knowing you're out there. Obviously, I'm bummed about this outcome, but I'm going for it in my own 'alternative' way now, because I wouldn't want you to say I traded my ass for a hole in the ground." Eight months later, her baffled surgeon, whom she referred to as "the Ass Man," told her, "I see no reason to remove your rectum... things look beautiful down there." T. told him "I think you're working too hard Doc. You need to get out more." Consequently, she invited him to come fly-fishing with her.

Five years after the surgery, T. wrote, "On the medical front – I guess that would be my back side – the Ass Man says it's even more beautiful than it was before, which means I am once again the perfect asshole."

At a deep, energetic level, when people come together to focus on an idea or pray for an individual, it has an impact. It's hard to explain this phenomenon with reproducible scientific data because it's hard to measure the effects of prayer. Since there are so many ways of doing it, it's hard to reproduce all the variables to make the results reliable. But when science defines the terms of the inquiry, it also defines its conclusions. The language of science is not the language of the human spirit, which doesn't lend itself to such measurements.

If it does your heart good to know that every day somewhere out there someone is thinking about you in a good way, pulling for you, wanting you to feel peace, comfort, and blessing, then go and seek it out. People will respond, and it has no bad side effects.

The important thing to remember is, if you have to be sure before you make a move, you may wait too long. Sooner or later all of us face something we don't know much about. We don't have to come from a place of certainty; we have to come from a place that feels right.

But what if your current life is devoid of ritual and ceremony? Look for kindred spirits in a community that utilizes them or learn how to create your own. At the soul level, we

are all tribal people. Rituals and ceremonies help bind us together in community.

My friend Elisabeth Kubler-Ross was a pioneer psychiatrist and champion for the terminally ill. She changed the way people talk to each other about death and dying. I knew her during the last 10 years of her life. Shortly after her move to Arizona, Elisabeth sustained her first stroke. A mutual friend told me she was concerned about Elisabeth's mental state because she was cursing God in 60 languages and railing against her incapacities. Our friend encouraged her to meet me, and I said I'd make a home visit.

Elisabeth lived way out in the desert, a sprawling ranch house with an Indian tipi in front of it. Bird feeders hung everywhere, while javelinas and coyotes wandered the grounds. When I first arrived, I called through the open screen door, and Elisabeth shouted back to come in. She was in a recliner, surrounded by books and mail that was stacked in piles on tables all around her. She offered me English breakfast tea and directed me to put the water on to make it. In her direct, opinionated, crusty style, she interrogated me about my German name and added that they were a humorless stock. We talked about Freud, Jung, my work with Indians, and my thoughts about an afterlife. After the interrogation, she answered my questions and invited me back.

Over the next decade, we established our own healing ceremony. I'd bring the bagels with cream cheese, lox and capers; she'd light up a Dunhill cigarette. We teased each other, laughed, commiserated, and sometimes quarreled. Our visits always ended with a goodbye treat – a piece of Swiss chocolate, which is much better than German.

She had another stroke, some serious infections, and system failures, but survived them all. Our breakfasts continued, Elisabeth still mentally alert and angry at God for bringing her so close to the flight home but always leaving her at the gate. Even while she was approaching death, she was doing what she had done better than almost anyone else – sharing the truth of her heart and shining a light on the process of dying. The week before she died, when it came time for our goodbye chocolate, Elisabeth said, "I'm giving it to you now, but I don't want you to eat it. Wait and eat it later." It wasn't clear to me what later meant, but I tucked it away in my office refrigerator. Her memorial service took place a month after her death over Labor Day weekend. I had planned to go on a fishing trip with my grandkids. I thought

Symbols, Rituals and Ceremonies

about staying home and attending but knew Elisabeth would've encouraged me to go.

I brought along that piece of Swiss chocolate she told me to save. Her memorial service was scheduled at 3:00 P.M. on Saturday afternoon. At that time, I reeled in my line and sat down on the riverbank. From my vest pocket, I took out the chocolate, opened the foil wrapper, and plopped the whole piece in my mouth. As it oozed, I looked up from the water's edge at the blue sky above and laughed thinking about Elisabeth's last teaching. Don't eat it now, wait till later. Save a piece of the ones you love for later – a piece of chocolate, a song, picture, or place where you touch the soul of those who've touched you. Every year on Labor Day, it is my ritual to eat a piece of Swiss chocolate to honor my friend's life.

I am a ceremonialist, and when a need arises, I find a way to participate in one. The need seems to arise more often as I get older. In the midst of this aging assault with more groaning in every organ system, I asked my beloved friend, Rabbi Gershon Winkler, to perform a healing ceremony for me. Gershon is the only rabbi-shaman I know. He is a distinguished Torah scholar who reads the Babylonian Talmud in its original Aramaic, and a Kabbalist teaching the lesser-known traditions of Judaism's rich mystical wisdom and Hebraic shamanism.

I stood outside on a high, desert plateau in New Mexico. The sun was coming down, and the crisp autumn air was infused with the scent of piñon pine. Rabbi Gershon drew a large circle on the ground, maybe 10 feet in diameter with a 7-foot-long, hand-carved walking stick. In the center of the circle, he drew mystical symbols of powers and guardian angels. Then he whispered in my ear, asking me to tell him what it was I wanted to heal. I told him about my awareness of my physical decline, my fear of losing control of my body, and my memory lapses.

Inside the circle, he drew ancient kabalistic symbols, which he explained and then handed me his walking stick. He showed me where in the middle of my chest to put one end of the staff and how to hold the other end just inches above the circle he had inscribed in the ground.

To the beat of his drum, which had hide covered by the same symbols, we started walking around the circle with me focusing on keeping the stick in the groove. Rabbi Gershon walked behind me whispering the Hebrew word, "Henainie," which means "Here I am," and telling me to repeat it after him. Round and round we walked. "Henainie, Henainie, Here I Am." Slowly, focusing on the path and the keeping the stick just an inch off the ground, I was in a walking trance acknowledging that indeed this is the only place I am.

After minutes, which seemed like hours, Gershon took my arm and lead me into the middle of the circle to stand amidst the symbols. He held out his

RABBI GERSHON

open arms and invited me to give the stick back to him. While he chanted, we passed the stick back and forth between us. Finally, he kept it and raised and lowered it in front of me, then walked around me and stood behind me. When he lifted the stick, the setting sun caused a shadow of the stick to appear on the ground in front of me. It was a snake, wriggling but not moving anywhere.

Gershon walked back in front of me and again handed me the stick and told me to hold the stick high and dance with him while he chanted. As I danced around, I saw the snakes shadow again but this time it was moving, not wriggling helplessly. In that Henainie moment, I understood that as long as I could still move, I did not have to focus on the steps I'd lost. Like Brenda, I asked him to comment, and this is what he said:

> *I can't add much to the story other than emphasize that the power of ceremony lies more in the person coming to the ceremony than in the one guiding it. If you do not bring yourself to the ceremony, it becomes meaningless, rote, and empty. This is why I had you recite over and over again, "Henainie -- I am here," to invoke your consciousness to be present in the moment, in the ceremony. The ceremony itself is a vehicle, a means of unblocking whatever it is that is impeding your life walk. Moses at the Burning Bush was told by the Creator, "Remove your sandals from off of your feet," which, in its original Hebrew, translates literally as, "Remove the lock from off of your patterns." Ceremonies shake us out of our stupor so that we might see with fresh eyes, walk with brand new feet, and feel with a new heart.*

In appreciation of that ceremony, I asked a friend who carves to carve a pendant in sacred Indian pipestone that incorporated the three Hebrew letters of the word, "Henainie." It's a beautiful keepsake that hangs on the fireplace in my office, reminding me to dance in every moment.

I've told this story to patients who have also struggled with their losses and fears and to whom I've lent it to aid in their recovery. Harry was crippled by anxiety and despair after recovering from bypass surgery at the age of 50. I helped him make some choices about his lifestyle, and Harry did well over the years. At 70, they put in a pacemaker to control his irregular heartbeat, after which he developed an infection that almost killed him. He got anxious and depressed again, and doctors put him on tranquilizing drugs, which made him less anxious but also sleepy, wobbly, and unable to breathe well

Symbols, Rituals and Ceremonies

at night. They discharged him on lots of medications, which ultimately left him confused and agitated. He was re-admitted to the hospital within a week because he became aggressively delusional. The psychiatrist who evaluated him wanted to put him on a potent antipsychotic medication to control his agitation and delusions; Harry thought she was trying to kill him and wanted to be discharged from the hospital. His wife told the doctor no more drugs until they spoke with me.

I told the psychiatrist of my long-term relationship with Harry over the years, and that I thought we might address his panic and agitation with more behavioral approaches rather than more medications. She said that she would discharge him AMA (against medical advice) if I would take full responsibility for his aftercare. He and his wife cosigned the release form that he was being discharged against medical advice. His wife brought him from the hospital to my office where we talked. He knew I wasn't going to kill him, so we talked and he calmed down. Looking around, Harry focused on the Henainie pendant on my fireplace and asked me about it. I told Harry the whole story of my fearful preoccupations, the ceremony Rabbi Gershon performed, and my Henainie moment. I told him that I hang it on the mantel to remind me to give up those ideas and behaviors that no longer serve me well.

> All symbols have power...Gather all those that move you as you journey through life so that you can feel their power when you need them most.

It was also clear at that moment that I should give it to Harry for a while. He wanted it, but I said it came with some instructions. First, when he would get up in the morning, he needed to perform a sunrise ritual of his choosing, which included saying, "Henainie, Here I Am, Thank you for this day." Then he was to carry it with him during the day, and at night, he was to hang it on the bedroom mirror. He could give it back to me when he was feeling better.

We saw each other often in those first weeks, and within a month, he was weaned from his anxiety drugs. We tapered our visits, but he carried the Henainie amulet around in his pants pocket for the next six months. By then, his heart rhythm was stable, he elected not to have another pacemaker, and he was back to work. I've since given it to others; I tell them the symbol's history, which of course now includes Harry's story.

All symbols have power. Medicines, robotic surgical arms, stones, feathers, drums and even amulets can contribute to healing. Gather all those that move you as you journey through life so that you can feel their power when you need them most.

Chapter 7

The Point of the Arrow

I was invited by the Huichol Indians, an isolated tribe living deep in Central Mexico's Sierra Madre Mountains, to help them eradicate an epidemic among the children that was caused by witchcraft. Accompanied by five colleagues, this astounding experience allowed me to cross the boundaries of culture and language to explore an aspect of my healing power that I had not previously owned. The power of that event also awakened forces within that threatened to consume me. When one opens channels into the unconscious mind and unleashes what C. J. Jung calls "the place of active imagination," it can get scary. Balancing the awakenings with my everyday realities and not getting hooked on the "Point of the Arrow," as the Huichol say, became the task.

It all started in a beachfront bar in La Paz, Baja, California. Watching the sun setting over the Sea of Cortez, I met Fernando Ortiz-Monasterio, a civil engineer, which created the right people, at the right time, at the right place. Upon hearing that I was a psychiatrist who worked with Native Americans, Fernando told me about a serious psychiatric problem he had encountered among the Huichols.

Fernando told me that the children in boarding schools, some as young as 5 years old, were hallucinating. It was attributed to sorcery. The children, thinking an evil spirit had possessed them, became incredibly strong and had to be physically restrained. If they got away, they could run for miles. There were also occasions when they became violent toward others. The problem had been going on for 10 years, and traditional shamans, called Marakame, had been unable to cure the disease. Some observers thought this might be the result of jimson weed intoxication. The cost of this illness, both psychologically and economically, had been devastating.

Fernando asked me if I'd ever seen such a problem, and I told him I had. I had seen spells caused by drugs and alcohol psychosis, hysteria, and witchcraft. In my experience, it didn't make any difference if the disease was explained genetically, psychoanalytically, psychopharmacologically, or by sorcery; the affliction was real and could be treated. He asked me if I thought I could be helpful, and I said, "Maybe... let's correspond."

After many e-mails, shared literature, and questions translated into Huichol and hand-carried into the villages, the boarding school principal sent an invitation officially asking for help. Fernando put together the Mexican team, which included his brother Pablo, a world-class photographer and author who had worked among the Huichol, and Marta Riveroll, who had previously worked among the Huichol and turned out to be a most extraordinary energy healer.

I organized the American team, which included John Koriath, a research psychologist and community organizer, and Joyce Mills, a talented play therapist, lecturer, and author. Joyce, John, and I had worked together in the Turtle Island Project integrating indigenous and Western healing traditions. Now, we educated ourselves about the Huichols. This ancient tribe calls themselves, Wixarika. They have lived in these mountains for at least 15,000 years according to carbon-dated ashes from their sacred fireplaces. The Huichols worship at the oldest, most continually-used ceremonial altars in all of the Americas. They were discovered and Christianized by the Spaniards and then essentially ignored because of their inaccessibility.

PABLO, DR. H, MARTA, JOYCE, FERNANDO AND JOHN

For more than a decade, students in boarding schools had been plagued by an epidemic of demonic possession. Children became possessed by a mysterious demonic "illness" that took over their bodies. They became incredibly strong and aggressive, roared like animals, and if they were not immobilized, would run away and attack people. Some afflicted children had even stoned a suspected sorcerer to death.

The Huichols have systematized their knowledge of the cause and treatment of disease. Their explanation for all illnesses not caused by old age is to be found in the supernatural. The exploration of these mystical realms is facilitated by the holy sacrament, hicuri, or peyote. Peyote is central to Huichol beliefs, and marakame are the trusted guides who unfold its mysteries. Many believe that a little hallucinogenic cactus, hicuri, is the manifestation of God's presence on earth. Hicuri is the way to enlightenment and health. During the year, small groups make the long, difficult, hundreds-of-miles journey to Wiricuta to gather this holy sacrament. It is the goal of every Huichol to make this pilgrimage because it is a stopping place on the road to eternity.

In traditional Huichol culture, spiritual pursuits and visionary experience are the central tasks in life. Huichols maintain tribal and planetary balance by celebrating a pantheon of ancestors and holy places. The marakame are the most highly respected leaders of the communities. The position seems to run in families, but it is also possible to be called to the work by the spirits.

> "In traditional Huichol culture, spiritual pursuits and visionary experience are the central tasks in life. "

Most are men, but there are a few female marakame. Learning to become a marakame takes many years. The successful candidate has to absorb an enormous body of knowledge, including the use of medicinal plants, and learn to recite compellingly the sacred stories and summon the help of spirits. Not a day goes by without a marakame making the time to connect with these ancestral spirits. The marakame know the deities well, and they are not afraid to serve as vehicles for their healing power. Sometimes they successfully conquer illnesses and sometimes not.

The Huichol believed the demonic illness was attributable to witchcraft and turned to their marakame to treat the problem. Many marakame were called but none could cure the illness. Medical doctors who staffed the local clinic prescribed drugs for what they believed to be a "psychotic" disorder. Psychiatrists were consulted, and some even visited and recognized it as a culture-bound syndrome that a shaman could treat. However, when told that it had been tried many times and failed, they offered no other solution.

The predominant opinion was that a sorcerer, who was a "man of kieri," caused the illness. Kieri, or jimson weed, is another hallucinogenic plant that, like hicuri, has enormous power. Hicuri is the light side of spiritual deliverance, and kieri has the capacity to reveal the dark side of the unconscious mind. Kieri has a dual personality; it holds a key to enlightenment, but it has the power to seduce you to the dark side of sorcery. In every healer, there is a potential sorcerer. When the ego overtakes the reality of one's flawed humanity and the healer wants to magnify his healing power, he succumbs to the black magic. Such a sorcerer can capture a person's life force, kupuri, and destroy him or her.

The fact that this illness was so pervasive and persistent in the boarding schools made us wonder about its manifestation as the dark side of compulsory education and its impact on traditional Huichol life. Was the illness a symptomatic manifestation of two opposing forces, the clash between traditionalists and modernists?

The traditionalists maintain the Huichol way of life and live in the same isolated villages their ancestors inhabited for thousands of years to guard the holiest Huichol sanctuaries. The traditionalists define the customs Huichols follow to live a long and healthy life. The progressive modernists live on the mesa-tops with access to electricity, running water, roads, landing strips, convenience stores, TVs, and computer games. Following the customs was getting harder in the new environment.

I had seen the manifestations of such clashes before, which frequently resulted in escalating violence, family discord, alcoholism, and addiction. I have discussed previously how the children are often the most vulnerable to manifesting psychological symptoms because they are in the middle of this struggle (The Dancing Healers, The Theft of the Spirit). Schools are the primary source of assimilation, and few tribal groups have survived compulsory education and remained culturally intact. It is impossible to build a wall of separation that will protect a culture from the allure of modernity. When this push and pull becomes so intense, and neither side lets the other win, both are "stricken by the arrow of disease." The Huichols needed somebody from the outside skilled in Western and traditional medical approaches to treat illness and bring them together.

I have seen such conditions, and they were curable when the healer could mobilize a power greater than the one causing illness. This is the basic principle of all psychotherapy. It does not matter whether you call the disease-producing mechanism a monster that possesses your body and mind or the incorporation of a negative introject. The treatment for such problems is to help patients and communities find the power to confront and overcome their demons.

The organizer and moving force was Fernando, who was intimately familiar with and accepted by the tribe. Over the last years, he had built a magnificent bridge over the raging waters of the Chapalagana River, which had swept away many children during the rainy season. Fernando was also instrumental in replenishing the dwindling deer population, one of the Huichols' sacred totemic animals. He was a trusted relative.

Fernando's brother, photojournalist Pablo, would document the healing process. Riveroll, a theologian by training and an extraordinary, intuitive psychotherapist and energy healer, had the exceptional ability to connect with the Huichols on previous visits. School Director Jesus Minjares Robles, a community leader, obtained all the relevant data from previous cases and negotiated access into the community.

Dr. Koriath, a psychophysiologist, whose area of expertise is in the heart/brain connection, and Dr. Mills, a child psychotherapist, joined me from the U.S. We knew each other well from the Turtle Island Project and came up with a rudimentary plan.

We'd involve all the children and ask them to draw a picture of what they thought the illness looked like, ultimately putting a face to the demon. We wanted to draw it out of them and use these pictures as the foundation of a sacred healing offering at the conclusion of our work. Joyce envisioned wrapping our offering in a shawl that she would commission her Navajo sister to make. The weaver, a member of the Native American Church, whose members also use the sacrament, said she would make two of them. She would make a big one for the offering and a smaller one to wrap around an afflicted child. I would bring a tape recorder to record our voices and songs, which could be played to the swaddled victim in case the symptoms recurred.

It was our hope to talk to parents, teachers, community members, and, if we could, a marakame. I would bring along my medical bag with some basic instruments to listen to hearts and look into eyes and ears along with some minor analgesics and herbal teas. To break down the boundaries, we planned to conduct an evening clinic during which we would see anybody with any ailment.

Although this was the basic plan, it was clear to us all that some things would reveal themselves and be woven into the experience. We all came with open hearts, a loving commitment, and an abiding belief that if we trusted in the wisdom of the unconscious, we would find a way to help create a new ending to the old symptomatic story.

It took six months to make the necessary arrangements and to get the formal invitations from the school principal, the head of the Parents Association, and the tribe before we flew to Guadalajara. On a humid afternoon in April, we greeted each other face-to-face. There were joyous hugs as we crammed

THE ONLY TREE IN THE COMPOUND. PHOTOGRAPH BY PABLO ORTIZ-MONASTERIO

into a Chevy suburban with our luggage and supplies on the roof. It was a 10-hour drive to Huejuquilla, the literal end of the road and gateway to Huichol country. Exhausted, we checked into the only hotel after midnight.

Whatever time we awoke was too early, but we had a breakfast date with the school principal who, in full costume, had come down from Nueva Colonia to greet us. Then, we continued with a four-hour drive on a pot-holed cattle track until we reached the mesa-top town of maybe 1,000 people. The town's health clinic was staffed by senior medical students, convenience stores, church, and big boarding school. Fernando drove into the fenced compound and parked under the only tree. The principal introduced us to Marcos, the head of the Parents Association, who would become our guide, interpreter, and counselor. We were shown to our 10-foot by 9-foot by 12-foot single room, which served as bedroom for us all and our evening clinic for the next three days. We began to unpack while word of our arrival

The Point of The Arrow

spread through the community.

Some kids watched us from behind the buildings and slowly inched closer. Joyce and her turtle puppet made friends while we unloaded the van. When the community gathered, the children were the first to welcome us, lined up in precise rows and most in traditional dress. They sang songs and clapped their hands, and we clapped back. The school principal introduced us in the Huichol language, which Marcos then translated into Spanish and Pablo into English. Everyone knew we were the doctors, the marakame from

THE CHILDREN LINED UP IN PRECISE ROWS IN TRADITIONAL DRESS. PHOTOGRAPH BY PABLO ORTIZ-MONASTERIO

North America, who came to heal the "illness."

With ubiquitous translations, Fernando introduced himself and told of his relationship to the Huichols. Then he told them about us and that we had worked with indigenous people in North America. He told them we had treated children with similar illnesses and said we had come at our own expense. He told them that our healing work would cost them nothing, but we needed their support in our efforts.

Next, Fernando introduced me, and I told them about myself, my tribe, my family connections, and my relationship with their holy sacrament, hicuri. I talked about the symptoms and explained that I had treated such things before. I told them that I came with respect and appreciation for their healing ways. I told them I knew many powerful healers had tried to cure the illness, but it continued to reappear. They were afraid of the illness and uncertain of the future, but I believed that the monster that inspired that fear could be defeated if we joined to face it together.

After I finished speaking, John and Joyce outlined the plan. John redefined

the concept of a hysterical conversion reaction, calling it an "inside-out disease." He explained that whatever darkness had gotten inside the victims' bodies and minds had to come out before the healing light could get inside. Joyce then explained how the children would draw

HEALING TOTEMS WERE PLACED IN THE NAVAJO PRAYER SHAWL. PHOTOGRAPH BY PABLO ORTIZ-MONASTERIO

a picture of the monster, and how we would collect them for our offering.

Then she held up a beautiful shawl that had been created by her Navajo relatives in North America, also users of the sacrament peyote. Her relatives had said they had blessed it especially for the children. She said we were going to use the shawl to wrap up our offering. John placed the shawl at the base of the tree and asked the assembly to help us in our work by bringing something that had helped them to heal in the past and to place it into the bundle. When we were finished with our work, we would take the bundle and offer it at a holy place.

Before closing, I said I knew many people had suffered, and I wanted to speak with anyone who was not feeling well. Each night I would open a clinic at our home and all were welcome. When I finished, nobody moved. Fernando came up to me and said, "They are waiting for you to sing. They want to feel your heart." They had heard my words, but they wanted to hear me pray and sing my songs. A marakame who could not sing was like a violin with only one string. I began to chant. Slowly, songs emerged, and we all sang.

We mingled, had dinner, and afterward, went to the school playground where we were formally presented to the elementary school children. We explained how they got sick, how something had gotten inside them, and that we were going to get it out.

Then I did a little David Copperfield magic that I had just learned. I told them I could get something inside of them, and they would not even feel it. I could blow something into their tightly closed fist without their ever feeling it.

CHILDREN DRAWING THEIR FEARS. PHOTOGRAPH BY PABLO ORTIZ-MONASTERIO

There were titters when I asked for a volunteer. One brave 7-year-old girl came forward. I showed her some ashes I had brought from our cooking fire. Fire is a sacred totem among the Huichol and the symbolic energy of life. I told the girl I could blow those ashes into her closed fist. "Do you believe me?" I asked. She did not answer, and I was not so sure myself. With marginal dexterity, I managed the sleight of hand to "blow" the ashes into her closed fist. When she opened her fist, she stared in amazement at the ashes in her palm and then walked around showing it to the others. I asked if there was still a skeptic out there, and an older boy wanted me to do it again. I invited him up and repeated the magic feat. They were all listening now.

The next morning, we would draw out the illness monster. The children would make a picture of what they thought the creature looked like. Joyce told them to think about it tonight; maybe it had a face or a body, maybe a symbol, anything they imagined it might be. She would bring the paper and crayons that they could keep. We said goodnight long after dark, and as we approached the front door to our quarters, there were people lined up for the evening clinic.

The entire next day, elementary and high school students drew their image of the illness. The pictures were accompanied with stories about the incredible creatures and designs. Some were ordinary animals, others were half-animal, half-human creatures, and some were plants. When the children finished drawing their fear, Joyce asked them to draw a picture of what made their hearts happy. Joyce knew this was an extremely important aspect of their healing process. Not only would the children's fears be taken or offered, but it was equally important they would be left with their own symbolic images of strength, which are often shrouded in the dark shadows of fear.

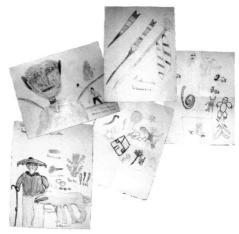

Photograph by Pablo Ortiz-Monasterio; Collage by Eric Jay Toll

One 9-year-old boy had depicted the illness as a giant cactus whose out-stretched limbs became arms with long, razor-sharp fingernails and flesh-tearing spines. He said the cactus monster wanted to tear open his chest and pierce his heart. He gave the monster the name, "Eutimio," which we later learned was the name of a well-known marakame who had been accused of being the sorcerer. This is a serious charge, and some members of the community thought he should be put to death. He was incarcerated for months in the tribal jail, but after investigation, was eventually released.

The village where Eutimio lived was a three-hour hike from the school down a steep canyon trail. We had hoped to speak with a marakame and wondered if a meeting with Eutimio could be arranged. We talked around the fire that night about how such a meeting might go. We would tell him about the boy's picture, without any finger-pointing or blame, and hope for his support and contribution to the offering. Marcos made it happen. Eutimio's son had been at the initial community meeting and news of our presence had already spread to the village. The next day, we got an invitation to meet with Eutimio.

On the way down, I talked to Marcos. Between my poor Spanish and his much better English, we managed to cobble a conversation together. Warm and open hearted, Marcos had returned to the village after years in Guadalajara.

Now married and with children at the school, I asked him what he thought was the cause of the illness. Marcos said there were many problems and the old customs were breaking down. The traditionalists believed the illness was punishment for federally-mandated elementary school education.

Families in the isolated villages of the Sierra Huichol were required to send their children away to school. For some, it was only a few hours walk, but for others it could be a two-day trek. Living away from their traditional observances was keeping more and more of them away for longer periods of time.

Marcos understood the argument because he had left home and learned the hard ways of the city before he came back to marry and have a family. He saw the manifestations of the loss of traditional influences, but he also was sympathetic to the progressive elements that wanted to avail themselves and their children of the opportunities of this new world. Marcos's view was that his people had survived the conquistadors. Their roots were deep, so he knew they would survive Coca-Cola and computers.

I asked Marcos if he believed the illness could be caused by a marakame's witchcraft. He knew people could become possessed and assured me this was not just a Huichol thing. "All Mexicans believe in the evil eye," he said. He did not believe one man could create such an illness. Then he added that Eutimio was no ordinary marakame. Marcos respected him and was a little afraid of him. He told me he was not sure if what we were doing would be helpful, but he believed it was possible because we came from the outside. We were doctors who understood both sides, and maybe we could bridge the gap. Then Marcos smiled and said, "Many people are watching you."

The walk down was like traveling through a time warp. We were high up on the cliffs when the village first appeared. I imagined that this is what the first outsiders must have felt when they discovered the Hopi mesas. As we got closer, Marcos pointed out the holy temples, which were surrounded by adobe walls separating the sacred grounds from the surrounding homes. There was a palpable energy here.

Eutimio's family compound was a large rancheria with at least five homes and its own religious sanctuary called a calihuey. He was 81 years old, had 14 children, 44 grandchildren, and 87 great-grandchildren. Entering his compound, we gathered under a tree where chairs, tree stumps, and blankets were arranged in a large circle. Women and children stood on the outside. I was invited to sit in one of the special marakame chairs. When we were seated, Euti-

DR. H. AND EUTIMIO. PHOTOGRAPH BY PABLO ORTIZ-MONASTERIO

The Point of The Arrow

mio was escorted out. He greeted us all and then sat next to me.

Marcos translated Fernando's Spanish into Nahual. He thanked Eutimio and his family for the invitation and said that we came with respect and honor for his reputation. Then he made the formal introductions and said I had worked with native people in North America and seen this disease before. We all came at our own expense and expected no payment.

Pablo translated for me in his passionate, soulful way. We told Eutimio how his name had been mentioned and that we were not here to point blame. Rather, we came to ask for his help in our efforts. We could see that the sacred balance between hicuri and kieri needed to be restored so that the Huichol circle could become whole again. We knew how much he and his family had already suffered and hoped that he would bless our work and consider making a contribution to our offering. And then, without invitation this time, we stood together and sang.

EUTIMIO'S ALTAR. PHOTOGRAPH BY PABLO ORTIZ-MONASTERIO

When we finished, I sat in a marakame chair next to Eutimio. He pointed to my Detroit Redwings baseball cap and motioned for me to give it to him. When I did, he took off his marakame's hat and gave it to me. I thought this was his offering, but he said it was for me. Then he stood up and invited Pablo and me to follow him into his calihuey. The three of us climbed up the few steps into the sanctuary, a small stone house with a thatch roof. Inside, there was barely enough room for the three of us to stand, much less walk around. The sanctuary was stuffed from floor to ceiling with sacred objects on tables, windowsills, and hanging from the roof beams. There were deerskins, painted deer skulls, feathers, masks, baskets filled with fetishes, stones, beads, peyote plants, Christian symbols, and a tiny key chain painting of him done by Diego Rivera.

EUTIMIO WITH RED WINGS CAP. PHOTOGRAPH BY PABLO ORTIZ-MONASTERIO

One table was crowded with baskets filled with carved wooden prayer sticks called muvieri. These sacred objects are potent healing fetishes. We watched Eutimio as he examined one after another until he found just the one that spoke to him. He then motioned for me to give him my new hat and proceeded to tie the muvieri onto it. This was his offering.

Before we left, he asked if I would look into his right eye. He was going blind and added that one side of his face had also been paralyzed for several years. I could see the facial asymmetry, but other than in his face, he had no other muscle weakness. The paralysis was probably the remnant of an old Bell's palsy that would not get any better or worse. When I looked into his eye, however, he had a dense cataract, which I told him could be improved with surgery.

It was late afternoon before we left, and Eutimio asked us to sing some parting songs. We sang hymns in English, Spanish, Hebrew, Ponca, Navajo, Lakota, Mohave, and Cree – the songs of many tribes and generations. Hearing their voices reverberating off the cliff walls moved me to tears. That tingling energy stayed with me on the walk out. Hearing those tunes humming in my brain lifted me from canyon floor to the rim almost effortlessly.

The next morning, we stood in a circle under the big tree around the Navajo shawl now filled with the children's drawings, decorated gourds, weavings, beadwork, peyote, a beaded deer skull, sacred Hawaiian salt, and flat-leaf cedar from the Black Hills of South Dakota. Many people were there just to see if I was still standing after my meeting with Eutimio.

Pablo related every rich detail of our meeting with psychodramatic flair. When he finished, he came to me and turned me around to show the assembly I was still whole. He then motioned for me to take off my hat and untie the muvieri, which I then gave to him. He walked it around the circle for everyone to see and then placed it into the offering.

Fernando held up the letter signed by the principal and Marcos, which described our work, our request of the tribal council to spend the night, and our plea to make this offering at the "Holy of Holies." At the end, we rolled up the offering and then held hands, sang closing blessings, and slowly walked around the circle to say goodbye to each and every person. To each child, we gave a small gift – a box of crayons, soap bubbles, and coloring books. The feeling of love was palpable.

After the ceremony, we drove on the only road to Santa Catarina, the capitol of the Sierra Huichol. It is a steep, one-lane trail, impassable in the rainy season. Before this road was completed just the year before, there was only a footpath in. Few non-Huichol visitors ever wandered in here. Even with the letter from the school principal and community, we knew there was little likelihood that we would be allowed to make our offering at their sacred source, the Holy of Holies. No more than a handful of outsiders had ever seen it, especially after the Norwegian explorer and naturalist, Carl Lumholtz, visited at the turn of the twentieth century and took one of their sacred altarpieces.

I forgot all about our reception on the ride down because I was holding the door handle in a death grip. In the dry season, the road is coated with a layer of fine powder, which makes you slide from side to side on the single lane. We were also headed directly into the setting sun. I was blinded, and we often slid perilously close to the unguarded edge on the hairpin turns. Seeing me white-knuckled, Fernando smiled and asked me why I was so tense.

Halfway down, I caught my first glimpse of the village. With pueblo-style adobe homes, a church, and a courtyard, it may be the oldest continuously-

'KWISE AROUND THE TABLE FROM LEFT; JOYCE, DR. H. PABLO, 'ANDO, JOYCE

inhabited community in all of the Americas. The road ended at a convenience store with a solar-powered refrigerator. We drove into the village, past the community water tank and spigot, and parked the van next to the community house. I staggered out and kissed the ground. The governor appeared, and Fernando delivered the customary introductions, and then read the letter. The governor listened, but we knew he had already heard the story. He said we could stay the night and that later they would decide at a council meeting whether or not we would be allowed in to make the offering.

We carried our stuff into the community house, a huge two-story structure. It was maybe 50-feet long by 30-feet wide and supported by three large center posts. An adobe bench surrounded the entire room.

Fernando had an old friend in the village with whom he had made arrangements for us to have dinner at his home. Fresh hand-pressed tortillas accompanied an exquisitely flavorful stew of indeterminate substance. Afterward, we strolled through the village. The beautiful church had been built three centuries before. In front of it was a walled courtyard that contained a life-sized statue of Christ. Dressed in a traditional peyotero's costume with long skirt and feathered headdress, it was stunning. The "Keeper of the Flame," who saw that the fire inside the church never went out, guarded the entrance.

Catholic priests conduct Mass here twice a year on Easter and Christmas, but the Huichols come here to pray on every important occasion, such as harvests, hunting expeditions, and pilgrimages to the sacred peyote gardens. They dance all night in the courtyard, stomping hard on the earth to awaken the spirits of their ancestors and ask them to keep their circle whole.

It was after dark when we were summoned to the tribal chambers. The council room was long and narrow. Inside the entrance, a high wooden table was set in front of an elevated adobe bench behind which all the council members sat. In front of the table was an open fireplace, and at the other end of the long room was the prison cell in which Eutimio had been incarcerated. The council members, men and women both young and old, some in traditional clothing while others wore blue jeans and t-shirts, passed around the letter of introduction.

Fernando told the whole story again – how we had come together, what we had done with the children, our visit with Eutimio, and his contribution to the offering. When he finished, a passionate exchange ensued replete with tears and angry outbursts. Some wanted to see what was inside the offering. Others did not because they were afraid that once opened, it might unleash a dark force, which would be the sorcerer's revenge for his incarceration. The discussion became so passionate that at one point I whispered to Fernando that we had other options. He whispered back that they had to go through this if the council was going to give permission.

When a consensus developed, the governor called the question, and they decided to open the offering. First, an official cleansed the entire chamber with Copal incense and waved the fragrant smoke over everyone and the closed offering bundle. Then he walked down to the jail cell where Eutimio

COMMUNITY HOUSE SLEEPING QUARTERS

had been held for months. Finally, they opened the bundle and purified its contents. The council carefully examined the children's drawings and Eutimio's muvieri. An official took pictures of the contents with a Kodak Instamatic.

More intense discussion followed, and then the governor turned to me and asked, "What did you see when you looked in Eutimio's eye?" When Fernando translated the governor's question, I thought it was a clinical question asking what was wrong with his eye. I responded that he had a cataract that was blinding him. Fernando clarified that the governor's question was not an anatomical one, it was one of soul. What did I see when I looked inside his eye? Could I see Eutimio's soul, and did I believe him to be sincere? Did I trust him? Was his muvieri a healing offering? I said I believed him; I believed he wanted this illness to end. He was an old man who had suffered much, as had his entire family. He did not want the memory of this illness to be his legacy,

The Point of The Arrow

and I believed both he and his offering were sincere.

More discussion ensued, and finally, they decided we could bury the offering at the Holy of Holies. The suffering had been so long-lasting and the need so critical that they agreed to let us go. However, it was with the proviso that six officials, including the governor and his wife, would accompany us, watch us perform the ceremony, and then escort us out. Finally, it was over. We were exhausted, and after washing up at the communal spigot, we slept side-by-side in our quarters.

I slept fitfully and was awakened from a dream in which I was on horseback. Startled by a hissing snake, the horse had bolted and I had been thrown off. But one foot had gotten stuck in the stirrups, and I had been dragged toward a precipice. It was hard to fall back asleep because the dreams had intensified by anxieties; the floor got harder and my uncertainties intensified. Among the ancient Jews, when the High Priest entered the Ark of the Covenant on the Day of Atonement to ask for blessings on behalf of the people, he went in with a rope tied around his ankle. If he was found unworthy by God to make this plea, he would be struck dead. Since no one else could enter that sacred space, they pulled him out by the rope. I was surely unworthy, but I would do the best I could and that would have to be sufficient.

DR. H INSIDE THE HOLY PLACE. PHOTOGRAPH BY PABLO ORTIZ-MONASTERIO

At daybreak, we gathered outside the community house. The governor came over and sat next to Fernando and me, and his mood seemed lighter. He said he had been dreaming all night. In his dream, he had seen Eutimio walking toward him, and they had approached one another until they were eye-to-eye. The governor had looked inside Eutimio's eye and said he, too, believed him to be sincere. I thought it a good omen for our trip.

We were led down by the tribal judge and followed by a policeman who carried a rifle. The descent was leisurely, but I knew the walk up would be harder. The deeper into the canyon we got, the more lush the landscape. It took an hour to reach the dry riverbed, which in a month would be a torrential river. Sitting on its bank, a dragonfly suddenly appeared in front of me. The dragonfly has mystical significance among Native people; among the Siletz band of Salish, the dead return as dragonflies, while among the Hopi, they are shamanic wizards whose complex eyes allow them to see the past, present, and future. I knew this would be no ordinary journey.

From the river, it is a short walk to the entrance to the Holy of Holies. The gateway is a serpentine cleft that splits a huge boulder. The crack is only big enough to let one person through at a time. The Huichol say the cleft was created by a giant snake that let them emerge there into their new world. We would be at the belly button of the Huichol world. This is their Temple Mount or Mecca.

Before we walked through, the judge stopped to pray. He asked for permission to enter, prayed for all of us, for the healing of the children, for the Earth and his people, and gave thanks to the Creator for all the gifts that had sustained them until now. Then he cut small twigs from a bush he said was the actual wood used by the Creator to make the first fire. He gave us each a few pieces and told us to offer it with our own prayers when we came to the Cave of Light.

It took only a minute to get through the crack, but during the short passage, I felt a cold shiver go through me. We prayed at the Cave of Light, each in our own way, and then moved on to more caves and pools, each one with its own altar and power. On either side of the trail, bushes were stuffed with fluffy, white, cotton puffs, the prayer offerings of generations of pilgrims. As the path became steeper, I had to hold onto the cliff walls, and as I did, I could feel a hum in the stones. I have felt this before in the Grand Canyon and underneath the Wailing Wall in Jerusalem when I touched the cornerstones of the First Temple.

And then suddenly, the altar and fireplace at the Holy of Holies opened up before us. It sits on a cliff ledge perhaps 30-feet wide and 100-feet long and faces a sheer, 100-foot wall. Ashes from the altar fireplace have been carbon-dated to be 10,000 to 15,000 years old, which makes this the oldest religious shrine in all of the Americas. We placed the offering in front of the altar and stood there quietly to take it all in.

The ledge is big enough to hold seven little calihueys or temples, each big enough for a single person. We each crawled into one. I stayed a while, prayed to be forgiven for my shortcomings, and hoped I would not have to be dragged out by my feet.

When I emerged, I walked over to an alcove that contained a pyramid of deer skulls placed there by pilgrims offering their prayers. I returned to the altar, entranced by the fireplace, the Guardians, and the smoke-stained cliff wall until Fernando tapped me on the shoulder and got me out of my reverie. He said it was time to pick out a place to bury the offering and that I should pick out a spot that spoke to me. There was a flat area on a narrow point near the cliff's edge that seemed right. That is where we dug the hole.

When we finished, we returned to the offering in front of the fireplace. We formed a circle around it, and I lit a cornhusk cigarette filled with tobacco given to us by our Navajo relatives. I spoke about its significance and the intention with which it was given to us.

Then, bending over the offering, I blew smoke all over it to open it up. I said I would pass the smoke around so each of us could take a puff, bless ourselves, and add our personal prayers for the healing work. In sharing our breath with each other in this way, we would speak as one voice, one heart, and one mind. I said what I said and stood in awe. We had done the best we could and asked that our prayers be heard and the sacred circle be made whole again. Everyone took a puff, said something, and passed it on until the smoke returned to me. I put what was left of the tobacco into the offering and then invited everyone to roll it up with me. We carried it to the burial pit and gently placed it in. I sprinkled the offering with water from the Spring of Life that flowed through the Holy of Holies, cedar from the Black Hills, and sacred salt from Hawaii. I recited the threefold final benediction in Hebrew and finished with some closing songs.

MAKING THE OFFERING. PHOTOGRAPH BY PABLO ORTIZ-MONASTERIO

We did not hang around long afterward. The governor's wife began giving signals that it was time for us to go. Before returning through the cleft, we stopped for lunch on a broad ledge overlooking the Cave of Light. When we had finished, the governor invited us to cross the riverbed and go into the cave. Inside the spacious cave were several flat ledges that could accommodate a dozen people comfortably. The walls were covered with glyphs and there were small altars in every crevice containing fetishes and candle remains. At one end of the cave, a deep cistern held perpetually fresh water.

From where we were sitting, we would be able to see a step-laddered series of seven waterfalls. The place was overwhelming in its intensity. Slowly, we all began to sing. I saw the faces of the children at the closing circle and could feel their sufferings and strengths. We sang "Amazing Grace" in three languages at this magical place, and with the sunlight peeking in, I not only heard the tune but could see the words bounce off walls like sparks. Thinking about that moment of spiritual clarity, the feeling of being one with all that is still gives me goose bumps and makes me shudder. I can bring myself into that consciousness when I want to experience deep contentment.

Before we left, Fernando called me over to the cistern where he scooped out water, poured it over my head, and took me as brother. We gathered our things and walked back through the fissure. The three-hour climb out was exhausting, alleviated only by thoughts of a cold beer at the journey's end. I had clearly emerged from the world of the sacred into the profane.

We rested, packed up, heard music, and walked to the church whose courtyard was now filled with dancing peyoteros who had just returned from their pilgrimage to the sacred peyote gardens in Wiricuta. We watched as they placed their sacrament at the feet of the skirted Christ in the courtyard. They danced, stomping their feet to speak to their ancestors and reaffirm their place and purpose in this world. The Huichols see themselves as the carriers of the light into humanity; a chosen people honoring a commitment to the Creator to keep open the channels to the mystical unconscious to heal themselves and the world.

We exchanged gifts and waved goodbye. I slept on the ride out.

In the months following our departure, some minor manifestations appeared. A couple of children became agitated but without violent outbursts. A year and a half after our visit, the Mexican team returned, welcomed and thanked by the community, but also were informed that the community had taken control of the situation, and no further external work was needed. This is the letter our colleagues sent us:

> Dear Brothers and Sisters,
>
> This is the rainy season. Travel is difficult, and instead of the dust of last year, we move through mud and roads that sometimes seem like rivers. We miss you, but feel your presence. Even the old truck started coughing in despair at your absence. We were greeted warmly in the village, just like old acquaintances. There is universal recognition of the radical decline in cases (only two or three mild cases), and the change is noticeable to all. The community has come together, and the Extraordinary Assembly (the highest authority in the community) appointed five marakame to serve as the guardians of the healing of the children. Support groups among friends and parents have been formed to address the children's needs as well. There is no question that the community senses the problem of the children is something from the past.
>
> The Navajo shawl you brought last year as a protective covering for sick children is no longer at the Nueva boarding school. It has found its way to another boarding school, where it is kept as a protective omen. In the Calihuey of Pochotita, we sang, performed blessings and presented gift. On our way home, we sang the Doors's "The End." We are grateful beyond words for our connection and the blessing of our work together.

While the illness for the children was disappearing, we started to experience our own illnesses. We were given a hint that this might happen before we left Mexico. The night before leaving, we celebrated in Guadalajara and we met Rocio. She is a naturopath and Fernando's guide on the Huichol spiritual journey. Rocio has worked among the Huichols for 30 years and runs a hospital/rehab facility for them in the city. Rocio told us that what we had just experienced was an initiation into our own power. With our new awareness, we became "points of the arrow," the place where shamans gain access to their unconscious minds, which magnifies their therapeutic power. But she cautioned us and said, "Be careful with what you take away from here because living in this state of mind could get you hooked on the point of the arrow." I didn't know what she was talking about, and asked her what she meant. Rocio said, "When you see the world from such an open channel into the mysterious mind, you may see things that you don't want to know and then drown in the wonder of its gift. If you cannot balance your new awareness with your outer reality, then the gift that has been given you will be taken away."

I still didn't quite understand, but it wasn't long after returning from the Sierra where we were opened to the healing magic of our collective unconscious that I began to. All of us, to varying degrees, became sick with life threatening catastrophes. We were possessed by illnesses and losses, possessed by our inability to defend against things bubbling up inside us.

I came back and got a serious sinus infection that settled in my chest. A routine x-ray found my thyroid was enlarged. It turned out I had a large tumor, which ultimately turned out to be a benign cyst. But it caused a serious confrontation about aging and mortality, which was ongoing. Each of my colleagues experienced their own life and death crises.

"don't take yourelf too seriously… give up control of what you never had control of anyway."

Four years after our visit, the disease had disappeared and the community healed, but we the healers did not emerge unscathed. Something happened to all of us down there. We were so totally involved in that energy, so opened to seeing life from this extraordinary, unrehearsed, free-flowing perspective, that all the material bubbling up consumed us. We could not separate ourselves from the unconscious awakenings to deal with our everyday realities. We, all in our own way over those four years, became ill, or as the Huichol call it, "hooked on the point of the arrow."

We became possessed by energy more powerful than anything we could do to defend against it. When you open yourself to the magic of cosmic awakening, sometimes things bubble up that you don't want to see. If you dwell on those things, the sound of your own wheels can drive you crazy because you lose your connection with your whole self. The task, when we are bombarded by an unrestrained access into the unconscious, is to hang on while it flows through you until you can find a way out of the swamp of your demons and find peace with who you truly are.

Healers are always faced with the dilemma of seeking to expand their healing powers without becoming seduced by them. The task is to wrestle with this mysterious, spirit world while maintaining support in your everyday reality. These powerful forces are part of our nature and indispensable in healing others and ourselves, but the task is in appreciating the magic of what you see without becoming possessed by it. If you live entirely in the unconscious, you become a sorcerer. You become hooked on the Point of the Arrow by arrogance, pride, and ego.

This is a story about healing. It's about opening channels into the mind so that you can see the familiar in new ways; it's about also the importance of ritual, ceremony, supportive community, connecting to things other than yourself that inspire hope. And don't take yourself too seriously...give up control of what you never had control of anyway.

Afterword

'm old and getting older. Old age is not a fixed point any more than a sunrise, sunset, or high tide. It happens over time, and even before it actually happens, you can see it. You can see the light before the sun rises, you can watch the sun set and the tides ebb and flow for hours. Everything in nature is in flux. We are always in a state of flow between where we've been and where we're going. If we can stay open and live in the Henainie or I-am-here moment, then where we are is where we're supposed to be. It's a place that we are seeing for the first time with new eyes.

It's hard for us to live in the moment because it requires letting go of all the moments that came before and ignoring those we anticipate next. We compare where we are to where we'd rather be. Those old tapes we carry playing who we need to be or what we have to do in order to feel good about ourselves take us away from the moment.

Aging is nature's way of forcing us to accept that the way it was is not the way it is. Getting old is the process of learning to give up the resistance to being in the moment and seeing our landscape from a new perspective. If we can't do that, we become dispirited and cannot age gracefully.

So far this is my story, but it's not THE story. Nobody gets the whole story; we keep on getting it and getting it. If we strive to appreciate being in the moment, the light of that awareness will kindle our spirit and propel us forward.

I wrote Kindling Spirit because I believe that if we share our stories, we can heal by learning something from each other. We used to tell stories around fireplaces and dinner tables, but we're doing that less nowadays. Today, we come around a new fireplace, the computer. I'm hoping that if we gather around it to tell our stories, we can create a healing world.

In the end, the journey of our lives is a journey toward love. Love is the greatest kindler of the human spirit. As we age, we learn to love everything more intensely because we become aware that the time we have to enjoy it may be brief.

I'm writing from the patio of my library as I watch the sun set and find myself doing that more lately because in its glow, I feel my spirit renewed. To all of you who walk the healing journey, I say thank you. I say this for all my relations. "Mi Takuye Oyacin."

FOR MORE INFORMATION ABOUT DR. HAMMERSCHLAG
OR TO ORDER HIS BOOKS AND RECORDINGS,
GO TO WWW.HEALINGDOC.COM
OR
DR. HAMMERSCHLAG
3104 E. CAMELBACK ROAD #614
PHOENIX, AZ 85016

Made in the USA
Charleston, SC
08 October 2012